The Financial Freedom Equation

Master Your Money and Spend Your Days Doing Work That You Love

BEN LE FORT

Dedication

Harrison, everything in this book including its royalties is for you...

Contents

Setting the table

One of the most common personal finance traps is not knowing when you have enough money to live life on your terms. Life is a constant trade-off between time and money. Many of us go to work every day, doing work we don't particularly care about in exchange for money.

The idea of financial independence or financial freedom is that one day we will have enough money that allows us to work less and enjoy life on our terms without sacrificing the lifestyle we've grown accustomed to.

The million-dollar question is, how much money do you need to become financially free? Not knowing the answer to this question can lead to an endless cycle of constantly needing "*more*". KNOW MY #

That's why I have a simple definition of what financial freedom means to me: **Doing work I love without ever worrying about how I will pay the bills.**
  LOVE this definition

This definition has become my mission statement with money. But it's still a bit vague. How will one know when one has enough money to do work one loves without ever worrying about paying the bills?

Being the economic geek that I am, I decided to turn my definition of financial freedom into an equation.

Financial freedom = (Investment income + income from work you love) > Your living expenses

Once I can reliably make enough money through passive income or pursuing my passions to cover my living expenses, I will be financially free.

That is a clear-off ramp to financial freedom.

What I love most about this personal definition of financial freedom is that, unlike the Financial Independence, Retire Early (FIRE) movement's definition of Financial Independence, which says you need to save 25 times your living expenses, this provides two different tracks to success:

1. **Investment income.** Accumulating financial capital through saving and investing, much like what is preached in the FIRE movement.

2. **Income earned from pursuing passion projects.** This relies on your "human capital" aka using your skills and talents to make money.

My definition of financial freedom is not about having enough money to "*retire early*" but putting myself in a position to aim my human capital at a business or work that I love.

Put simply, it has allowed me to build a clear off-ramp from a full-time 9–5 worker who is obsessed with saving every penny to spending my days working on projects I care deeply about, even if they aren't always very profitable.

In this book, I'll give you the road map to achieve financial freedom. To be clear, this is not a magic solution or some kind of get-rich-quick scheme. Reshaping your finances takes a lot of time and hard work. **This is your road map, but you still need to walk the path yourself.**

The book is broken out into two parts.

In Part 1, you will learn the 10 things you need to know to be great at managing money. This is critical because, without proper money management skills, attaining financial freedom becomes nearly impossible. The quicker you master these skills, the sooner you will reach financial freedom.

In part 2, you are going to learn how to solve the financial freedom equation. You will learn that financial freedom comes down to three simple numbers: making money doing work you love, passive investment income, and your cost of living. I will introduce you to the 10% rule, which is your guide to achieving financial freedom in less than 10 years.

Part 1:

The 10 Things You Need To Know To Be Great With Money

Chapter 1:

To Be Great with Money, You Need a Powerful "Why"

You can know everything there is to know about paying off debt, saving and investing, or anything to do with money, but it means nothing if you don't have the right mindset.

When I say the right mindset, you simply need to believe that you can succeed with money. If you don't have hope that things can get better than they are today, you will be far less likely to be financially successful.

I believe that the most crucial factor in developing the right money mindset is to have a powerful "*why*".

Managing money is simple

Here is the truth: Managing money is not as complicated as you might think. As you will learn in this book, managing money is pretty simple.

To have a successful relationship with money, you don't need to be an "expert". You don't need to follow news about the stock market or what's happening in the economy. In fact, it's probably best if you tune all that type of information out completely.

To be successful with money, here is all you need to do:

- Have a system in place to monitor your spending.

- Put an emergency fund in place.

- Follow a proven method to pay off debt.

- Put your money into proven investments for the long term.

- Set up a simple DIY retirement plan.

- Create a budget that locks in your goals.

That's it.

Managing money is simple.

Managing money is hard

If managing money is so simple, then why do so many people struggle with their finances?

Because managing money is hard.

Managing money is both simple and hard. It's simple because all you need to do is follow the steps I listed above. It's hard because knowing what to do is meaningless unless you follow through on it day in and day out.

Personal finance has a lot in common with personal fitness.

- Getting in shape is very simple. All you need to do is eat healthy food and exercise.

- Getting in shape is also very hard. Junk food tastes better than broccoli, and exercising is exhausting.

Managing money has the same problem. Meeting a friend for lunch every day and going to the mall to buy things is more fun than packing your lunch and setting up automatic transfers to your investment account.

So, we have established that managing money is both simple and challenging. The question remains how do we bridge the gap?

You need a "why"

If managing money is simple, but accomplishing those simple tasks is hard, the solution to developing a better relationship with money is to ensure we accomplish those simple tasks.

We need to follow through on those tasks every day. Even when we are faced with the easier route, we take the hard route and accomplish those simple tasks.

It is easier said than done.

- Every time you leave your house or open your phone, someone is trying to sell you something.

- For many of us, when we hang out with friends and family, there is often pressure to spend money.

- If you are a parent, advertisers will make you feel like a bad parent if you don't buy the most expensive brands for your kids.

All day, every day, you will feel pressure to give your money away to other people. And every dollar you spend on something that brings no value to your life is a dollar that is not being used to pay down debt or invest.

If you don't have a strong "why", you're going to cave under that daily pressure and start using your money in ways that move you further away from where you want to be.

The first question you need to ask yourself is: **why is it worth it for me to improve my finances?**

Your "why" must be more powerful than your fears and doubts.

Money is a scary subject for a lot of people. A little bit of fear around money is healthy, but that fear has turned into daily anxiety for a lot of us.

Fear can lead to financial paralysis—when your money problems scare you so badly that it immobilizes you from addressing the issue.

When I was in my 20's, I was filled with so much financial anxiety that I could not bring myself to open up my monthly student loan statements.

I did not believe at that time that I would ever be able to pay that loan off, so I entered a depressed state where I thought to myself, "Why bother?" That financial paralysis led to me missing payments, accruing penalties and interest, and damaging my credit.

Financial fear and paralysis are toxic. It was not until I found my "why" that I found the courage to push past the fear and address my money problems head-on.

An example of a terrible "why" is: I want to be super rich.

If the reason you want to be successful with money is to become "rich", you are doomed to fail. Don't get me wrong; being rich and having nice things feels good. It might even be great motivation to get you started down the path of managing your finances.

However, it won't be a strong enough motivation to stay committed for the long run.

Another common "why" is family.

My experience has been that family is the best "why".

In 2012 I was $50,000 in debt while completing my Master's degree. I worked two jobs and still had to extend my student loans to help family members pay the bills. To say I was walking a financial tightrope would be an understatement.

If my motivation was to be "rich" and drive a fancy car and live in a big house one day, I am sure that I would not have made it through that year. The only reason I was able to pull through was that I had people I love that were depending on me. In other words, I had a powerful "why". That "why" meant that I was willing to do whatever it took for as long as it took to turn things around.

Which I did.

Eight years later, I had completed my master's degree and started a successful career and a profitable side-business that I am deeply passionate about. My wife and I can invest more money every month, and we were even able to buy a house for family members to live in.

I wasn't able to do this because I am some type of outlier or possess some special knowledge that no one else does, I was able to do it because day in and day out, I did the simple but hard things that needed to be done. I could sustain that over the long term because I started with a powerful "why"— family.

What's your "why"?

The easiest part about managing money is the technical aspect, like the most efficient way to pay off debt or how to build an emergency fund. The more complex and more powerful part of becoming successful with money is developing the right money mindset.

Step one in building a solid money mindset is to find a powerful "why" that will make the sacrifices required to turn your finances around worth it to you.

The right "*why*" must be more powerful than your fears or self-doubts. For that reason, focusing on all the nice things money can buy is a weak "*why*". I have found that family is my most powerful reason to become a great money manager.

The question you have to ask yourself is, "*What is your why?*"

Chapter 2:

How to Track Where Your Money is Going

The first thing you need to do to become great at managing money is to track your spending. While it takes some effort, tracking your expenses is a simple process.

Tracking your spending is a four-step process:

1. Gather all your bank account statements, credit card statements, and receipts for cash purchases. You'll need at least 30 days' worth of expenses.

2. Categorize all your monthly expenses.

3. Use either an expense tracking app or a spreadsheet template.

4. Evaluate where your money is going and use that information to change your saving and spending habits.

1. Gather all your receipts and account statements

The first step to tracking your expenses is to gather up the records of all your monthly expenses. There are three places you will find these records:

i.   The monthly statements for all your bank accounts.

ii.   The monthly statements for all your credit cards.

iii.   Receipts from any cash purchases.

These records will give you all the information you need to track your spending, including the following:

- Date of each purchase.

- Price.

- Details of each transaction such as name of store, and sometimes even the names of items purchased at the store.

It's also important to remember that you are not only tracking your spending on things you buy, but you are also tracking every penny. That means any fixed costs like rent or insurance and any money put toward paying off debt or saving.

2. Categorize all your monthly expenses

I believe in keeping things simple. Rather than having a dozen or more categories for your expenses, I recommend you categorize every penny into one of the three categories below:

1.   "The big 3."

2.   Values.

3.   Stuff.

- The average person spends between 50%-60% of their money on housing, transportation, and food. Together these expenses make up "the big 3". The big 3 can also include any expenses you consider to be "essential" like internet and phone costs. We will dive deep into everything you need to know about the big 3 in the next chapter.

- "Values" are the things that you spend money on that have a real impact on your life. Traveling, giving to charity, and investing in yourself are some examples of value expenses.

- "Stuff" is any non-essential spending that does not make you happy or provide any lasting impact. These can be big purchases like buying a new flat screen TV, or they can be small, like buying a pack of cigarettes.

3. Use an expense tracker app or spreadsheet

If you Google "*free expense tracker app*" or "*free expense tracking spreadsheet*", you are likely to find many great options. For the remainder of this chapter, I am going to discuss

tracking your expenses using the expense tracking spreadsheet I created. You can access the expense tracker for free at the URL in the footnote at the bottom of this page[1].

This spreadsheet has a particularly unique feature in that it tells you how many hours you had to work to pay for each expense. By thinking about the true cost of the things you buy in terms of time instead of money, it might help to clarify if you are happy with where your money is going.

Calculating your hourly-take home pay

To determine how many hours you need to work, for each expense, you need to calculate your hourly take-home pay. To do that, you'll need to know what your take-home pay is on each paycheck. So, grab your most recent pay stub, which probably looks something like this.

PAYMENTS		DEDUCTIONS		YEAR-TO-DATE	
REGULAR PAY	$2,500.00	FEDERAL TAX	$492	REGULAR PAY	$6,396.00
ADDITIONAL PAY		FEDERAL MED TAX	$207	ADDITIONAL PAY	$2,691.00
OTHER		Pension Contribution	$125.00	FEDERAL TAX	
OTHER		OTHER		FEDERAL MED TAX	

TIME OFF BALANCES			
VACATION		PERSONAL DAY	
SICK LEAVE		MEDICAL LEAVE	

TOTAL GROSS PAY	TOTAL DEDUCTIONS	TOTAL NET PAY	
$2,500.00	$824.00	$1,676.00	

Your total net pay or take-home pay is equal to your gross pay minus all taxes and deductions. It is the amount that hits your bank account on payday.

---

[1] The URL where you can download the expense tracking spreadsheet: https://dogged-mover-9757.ck.page/d756b9abe0

Once you know how much you clear on every paycheck, you simply need to divide that number by the number of hours you worked during that pay period.

As an example, let's assume the following.

- You clear $1,676 per paycheck.

- You get paid every two weeks.

- You work 40 hours per week.

That would mean you have an hourly take-home pay of $20.95. The expense tracking spreadsheet I use crunches those numbers for you.

Inputting your expenses

Once you have gathered all your receipts and account statements and calculated your hourly take-home pay, it's time to start inputting your expenses.

To get a complete picture of your expenses, you'll want to input the following information for every expense:

- The date of the expense or purchase.

- The dollar amount of the expense.

- A description of the purchase. This will help you understand what the expense was; for example, you could input "rent" or "coffee".

- Context of the purchase. This is particularly useful in determining if an expense should be classified as "values" or "stuff". For example, coffee might be classified as "stuff" if you bought it because you forgot to brew your own. On the other hand, if you purchased a coffee while catching up with a close friend, that might be classified as "values".

- Classification. Classify the expense as big 3, values, or stuff.

4. Evaluate where your money is going

Once you have inputted all your expenses into the expense tracker, it will look something like this:

Monthly Expense Tracker

		Total Money Spent	Total Hours of Your Life Given in Exchange
Big 3		$ 2,239.00	107
Values		$ 850.00	41
Stuff		$ 550.00	26

Add Expense

Date of purchase	Amount of purchase ($)	Description of purchase	Context of purchase	classification	Total Hours of Your Life Given in Exchange
	$1,249.00	Rent		Big 3	59
	$99.00	Utilities		Big 3	5
	$500.00	Car Payment		Big 3	24
	$400.00	Groceries		Big 3	19
	$100.00	anniversary dinner		values	5
	$500.00	Airline tickets		values	24
	$550.00	Random purchases		stuff	26
	$50.00	debt repayment		values	2
	$200.00	retirement savings		values	10

The expense tracker will tally up all your expenses and tell you how much money you spent on the big 3, values, and stuff. More importantly, it will show you how many hours you had to work to pay for those expenses.

In this example:

- $2,239 spent on the big 3 means you would need to work 107 hours to pay for these expenses based on the $20.95 per hour take-home pay calculated in step 3.

- $850 spent on values means you would have to work 41 hours.

- $550 spent on stuff means you would need to work 26 hours.

The same calculation is made for each individual expense you enter. This way, you can easily see that the true cost of your car payment is not $500; it is the 24 hours you need to spend at work to make that car payment.

Use this information to make changes

Once you figure out where your money is going each month, and you learn how many hours you are giving up for the things you buy, you simply need to ask yourself if you are satisfied with your results?

- If the answer is yes, then odds are you are pretty happy with the current state of your finances.

- If the answer is no, then it's time to identify the source of the problem.

The low-hanging fruit would be to minimize the amount of money spent on "stuff". Redirecting money from "stuff" to "values" is a good first step.

However, if you want to get serious about saving more money, the odds are that you'll need to reevaluate how much money you are spending on the big 3 as they account for the majority of your budget.

- If you have rooms in your house you're not using, you might consider renting them out to generate income or downsizing your home.

- If you're a two-car household, ask yourself if you would be willing to become a single-car household.

- If you're shocked about how much you are spending on groceries, you might consider making a weekly meal plan based on what is on sale at your grocery store.

The more money you can save from stuff and the big 3, you can be redirected to things you value. These can be "financial values" like paying off debt or "personal values" like traveling more often.

If you're only spending a fraction of your income on things that you value, odds are you are not living an intentional life. The goal should be to align your money with your values as much as possible.

Chapter Recap

- If you want to turn your finances around, the first thing you need to do is track your expenses and figure out where your money is going every month.

- Start by compiling the records of all your expenses, including bank and credit card statements, in addition to receipts from any cash purchases you make.

- Next, you'll need to define how you will categorize your expenses. I like to keep it simple and categorize all expenses as the big 3, values or stuff.

- Then you will need either an app or spreadsheet to organize your spending and present it in a way.

- To understand the "true cost" of the things you buy, don't look at how many dollars something costs but how many hours of your life you had to give up to buy that thing.

- Then it's simply a matter of inputting all your expenses (at least 30 days' worth) and evaluating the results.

- Ask yourself if the way you're spending your money makes you happy and helps you lead a fulfilling life. If the answer is anything but a resounding "yes", you know you have some work to do.

Chapter 3:

Managing the Big 3 Living Expenses

One of the most common pieces of financial advice I hear is to focus on cutting out small everyday purchases as the best way to save money. The argument is that seemingly small and routine purchases like buying coffee can add up to large sums over time.

While it is true that cutting out small purchases and spending less money on "*stuff*" can add up to meaningful amounts of money over your life, these small purchases are not costs you need to control if you want to save money.

If you want to save money, you need to start with your largest expenses in life, not your smallest.

Let's discuss why making smart choices around your big 3 living expenses is the easiest way to save more money.

What are the big 3 expenses?

The three biggest living expenses, or as I call them "the big 3" are:

1. Housing

2. Transportation

3. Food

Housing, transportation, and food account for more than 60%[2] of the average household budget. I am assuming that is more money than your daily coffee run costs. If you are looking to save more money, *the big 3* is an excellent place to start.

Let's have a look at how much money the average person spends on the big 3.

1. Housing

Housing is most people's most considerable expense. Housing costs account for 37% of after-tax household income in America. That means 37 cents of every dollar you bring home goes toward housing costs.

Let's focus on the cost of owning a home because it has a lot more hidden costs compared to renting.

When homeowners budget their housing costs, they typically account for predictable expenses.

- Mortgage payments
- Property taxes
- Home insurance
- Homeowners Association (HOA) fees
- Utility bills like electricity and heat

---

[2] *CONSUMER EXPENDITURES MIDYEAR UPDATE--JULY 2019 THROUGH JUNE 2020 AVERAGE.* (2021, April 29). U.S Bureau of Labor Statistics. https://www.bls.gov/news.release/cesmy.nr0.htm

There is a whole other category of unpredictable costs associated with owning your own home that most people fail to include in their budget.

Mandatory maintenance

One of the major perks of renting is that when something breaks or needs to be repaired, you can call your landlord.

When you own a home, you are on the hook for those repair costs. The average homeowner spends $2,016 per year or **$168 per month on general maintenance costs**[3].

A common rule of thumb is for homeowners to budget at least 1% of the value of their home for annual maintenance costs. If your home is worth $400,000, you will budget at least $4,000 per year or $333 per month for home repair costs.

Home Renovations

As a culture, we are obsessed with home renovations, and it is hitting our wallets. One report found that in 2018

---

[3] Statista. (2020, November 6). *Average monthly maintenance costs for homes U.S. 2017, by type.* https://www.statista.com/statistics/748004/average-monthly-maintenance-costs-for-homes-usa/

homeowners spent an average of $6,649 on home reno-vations[4]. That works out to nearly $555 per month.

Remember, these are renovations and upgrades. So, that $6,649 is in addition to the $2,016 spent on simple home maintenance.

Other hidden costs of homeownership

There are a lot of other costs associated with owning a home that people tend to forget about.

- Landscaping
- Snow removal
- House cleaning
- Security systems
- Pool maintenance

The average homeowner spent $638 or $53 per month on these services in 2018[5].

2. Transportation

I'm not a "*car guy*" and I have never really understood the appeal of car culture. So, I have never been able to wrap

---

[4] *2021 True Cost Report - HomeAdvisor.* (2021). Home Improvement Tips & Advice from HomeAdvisor. https://www.homeadvisor.com/r/true-cost-report/

[5] *Have You Budgeted for Unexpected Home Maintenance Costs?* (2018). The Balance. https://www.thebalance.com/average-homeowner-spending-on-maintenance-costs-4160279

my head around why people spend so much money on their cars.

While housing accounts for a larger share of household spending, cars are a bigger money pit. If you buy a house, you are going to spend more money on your home. However, you will at least own an asset that is likely to increase in value over time. When you buy a car, you are spending a lot of money on something that will eventually be worthless.

The monthly costs of buying a new car

When you buy a new car, here are the average monthly costs to keep that car on the road.

- Car payment: $555
- Insurance: $100
- Gas: $150
- Maintenance: $100
- Registration fees: $12

The total monthly cost of owning a new car: $916[6].

Once you throw in parking, the monthly cost of car ownership easily climbs over $1,000 per month.

---

[6] Reed, P. (2021, June 25). *What Is the Total Cost of Owning a Car?* Nerd Wallet. https://www.nerdwallet.com/article/loans/auto-loans/total-cost-owning-car

Depreciation

If you think your monthly car payment is the largest single expense of buying a new car, you would be wrong. The single biggest cost of new cars is depreciation.

Depreciation refers to the value your car loses the second you drive it off the lot.

What is the average cost of depreciation of a new car? According to CarFax, a new car depreciates by 20% in the first year you own it and 10% each of the next four years[7].

If you bought a brand new, $40,000 car, it would lose $8,000 in value in the first year after you bought it. That works out to $666 per month.

Spending more money than you need to on a brand-new car is an easy way to drive your finances into the ground.

3. Food

According to the U.S Bureau of Labor Statistics, the average American household spent $7,203 or $600 per month on food in 2018[8]. That works out to nearly 13% of take-home pay.

---

[7] Popely, R. P. (2021). *Car Depreciation: How Much It Costs You.* Https:// Www.Carfax.Com/. https://www.carfax.com/blog/car-depreciation
[8] *CONSUMER EXPENDITURES--2019.* (2020). U.S Bureau of Labor Statistics. https://www.bls.gov/news.release/cesan.nr0.htm

The total money spent on food includes food at home (groceries) and food away from home (eating out).

- $4,049 or $337 per month was spent on groceries.
- $3,154 or $262 per month was spent on eating out.

Reducing spending on the big 3 expenses

By now, it should be abundantly clear that controlling our spending on housing, transportation, and food is going to help you save a lot more money than cutting out your daily latte.

The question remains, how can you reduce the amount of money you spend on the big 3 expenses?

Let's dig into the question by discussing ways to save on each of the big 3 expenses, one at a time.

The simple solution to reducing housing expenses

Let's start with housing, which, as we covered, is most people's largest expense in life.

We all know housing costs have increased significantly, and they seem to keep going up every year. How can you reduce your housing costs if the prices keep going up? To answer that, we need to look at the reason housing costs are going up.

Here is a fact that might blow your mind. Adjusting for inflation, **the average housing cost per square foot has only increased by 4.6% in the U.S between 1973–2015[9]**.

The main reason housing costs have increased so much is that people want to live in bigger houses.

- In 1973 the average house size was **1,660** square feet

- In 2015, the average house size was **2,687** square feet

The average home was 62% bigger in 2015 than it was in 1973. What makes this even more expensive is that we have fewer people living in our giant houses.

- 3 people occupied a house in 1971

- Only 2.5 people occupied a house in 2015

Houses are nearly two-thirds larger, and we have 16% fewer people living in them than we used to. As a result, the number of square feet per person has nearly doubled.

- In 1973, the average house had 551 square feet per person.

- In 2015, the average house had 1,058 square feet per person.

---

[9] Perry, M. (2019, August 28). *New US homes today are 1,000 square feet larger than in 1973 and living space per person has nearly doubled.* American Enterprise Institute - AEI. https://www.aei.org/carpe-diem/new-us-homes-today-are-1000-square-feet-larger-than-in-1973-and-living-space-per-person-has-nearly-doubled/

And we are mystified about why housing costs have increased so much.

The simple solution to cutting your housing expenses should be obvious; downsize your home!

I know that's probably not what you want to hear. But did you think I was going to tell you the secret to saving money is buying a big house that you don't use?

The worst advice anyone ever gave me about real estate was to buy more house than I need today because "I'll grow into it". If you buy a house and you have an empty room, think about all the costs to maintain that room.

- Additional property taxes
- A larger mortgage
- Higher utility bills
- Higher maintenance and renovation costs

If you want to save more money, live in the smallest home you are comfortable living in. Which is probably smaller than you are thinking it is right now.

A more aggressive way to cut back on housing costs

If you are willing to make a more considerable sacrifice than merely downsizing, you could cut your monthly housing costs all the way down to $0 or even have your house provide positive cash flow.

Let me introduce you to the concept of *"house hacking"*.

House hacking is a pretty simple concept. The idea is to find a way to generate enough income from your primary residence to offset your personal housing costs.

How great would it be if someone else was paying your mortgage, utility bills, and property taxes? Do you think you would be able to save more money than you are today?

That is the appeal of house hacking and why it is so popular in the Financial Independence, Retire Early (FIRE) community. If you can eliminate your largest expense in life, saving money and building wealth gets a whole lot easier.

There are a number of different ways you can pull off a house hack.

- Rent out a room in your house.
- Rent out your entire house on Airbnb when you are out of town.
- Buy a multi-family property while living in one unit and renting out the others.
- If you rent and live alone, taking on a roommate is even a form of house hacking.

Whether you choose to downsize or house hack, there is a sacrifice that needs to be made. Downsizing involves giving up living space, while house hacking involves potentially giving up privacy.

You need to figure out which sacrifices are worth making, given your goals and preferences. The main point is that you probably need to think a lot more about your housing costs than you currently are.

Reducing transportation expenses

We have already covered that the monthly cost of owning a car can be as high as $1,000 per month. That is a lot of money.

Here is the simplest solution to reducing your transportation costs: **don't own a car!**

If you are struggling to save money and you don't absolutely need to own a car, consider selling it and buying a transit pass. Yes, this would require a sacrifice. Cars provide a lot of convenience and make getting around a lot easier. They are also one of the biggest money pits in life.

Whether you decide to own a car or not, there will be an opportunity cost.

- The cost of owning a car is all the money you need to spend to buy that car and keep it on the road.

- The cost of not owning a car is the lost convenience of moving from Point A to Point B as quickly and efficiently as possible.

You need to decide which cost is worth paying at this point in your life. If you have three kids, the financial cost of owning a car is one you may gladly pay.

If you don't have kids and you live in a city with a decent transit system, the amount of money you'll save by selling your car will likely outweigh the opportunity cost of getting around town less efficiently.

There is a reason we refer to managing our money as "*personal finance*". The answer to nearly every financial question is largely dependent upon our personal preferences and circumstances. There are very few answers to a personal finance question that universally applies to every person.

Returning to the family that includes three kids. It might be a no-brainer decision for that family to own a car. But do they need to have two cars? If they went from a two-car family to a one-car family, would the financial savings be worth it to them? Maybe and maybe not. However, it is a discussion that any family with three kids and two cars should be having.

I'm not saying you shouldn't own a car. I am saying that you absolutely need to be thinking about the opportunity costs of owning a car vs. not owning a car. Most people don't think about the decision to buy a car in this context, and it can cost them a lot of needless financial headaches.

Buy the crappiest car you are comfortable driving

If you have considered the opportunity cost and decided that, yes, it is worth it to you to own a car, the next decision you need to make is how much should you spend on your car?

Here's my advice; buy the crappiest car you are comfortable driving.

To be clear, when I say "crappy", I don't mean an unsafe car. I mean the safest, fuel-efficient, boring car for the lowest price possible, meaning don't go buy a brand new Mustang when a three-year-old Toyota gets the job done.

Remember the two biggest expenses of buying a new car.

1. The monthly payment
2. Depreciation

If you buy a new sports car or another expensive car, you are going to have a high monthly payment, and you are going to be paying a lot of depreciation.

If you buy a $40,000 car with all the bells and whistles, that car is going to begin losing value the second you drive it off the lot. Sooner or later, that $40,000 car will be worth nothing.

Do you know what most people do when that happens? Buy another $40,000 car and start the process all over again.

That's financial insanity!

Part of the reason people buy expensive cars is that they can easily get a car loan. Many people believe that if the bank is willing to lend them $40,000, that means they can afford a $40,000 car.

Car loans are a financial trap.

If you can't afford to buy your car in cash or you would prefer to invest that money, then a car loan makes sense. The problem for most people is that car loans trick them into thinking they can afford a more expensive car than they can. That's why so many people end up spending more on their monthly car payments than they save for retirement.

There is nothing wrong with buying a cheap, dependable, boring car. Stop worrying about looking cool and start worrying about where your money is going every month.

Generate cash with your car

If you want to get really aggressive with cutting back your transportation costs, you might consider the possibility of using your car to generate some cash.

There are two ways you can do this:

1.   Use your car to drive for Uber/Lyft or other ridesharing or food delivery companies.

2.   Rent your car on Turo or other car-sharing apps.

We are right back to the concept of opportunity cost. Driving for a ride-sharing company can help bring in extra money to offset the cost of owning a car. However, that income comes with two costs:

1.   The commitment of your time.

2.   Faster depreciation of your car through increased mileage.

Renting your car out on a ride-sharing app is another way to bring in additional money to offset the cost of owning a car. However, it also comes with two costs:

1.   Faster depreciation of your car through increased mileage.

2. The risk that whoever rents your car totals it and any potential associated liability.

These are not options that will work for everyone. Again, you need to weigh the opportunity costs and make the decision that works best for you.

Reducing food expenses

Finally, we come to food which is most people's third-largest expense and the expense we can most easily control. Making changes to where we live and how we move around takes time, but what we eat and how much we pay for food is something we can change immediately.

Cook your own food

The simplest way to reduce the amount of money you spend on food is to minimize your cost per meal. If you want to bring down your cost per meal, you need to buy your own groceries and prepare more of your food at home.

According to a report from Priceonomics[10]:

- It costs nearly five times more money per serving to eat at a restaurant than cooking the same meal at home.

---

[10] *How Much Money Do You Save by Cooking at Home?* (2018, June). Priceonomics. https://priceonomics.com/how-much-money-do-you-save-by-cooking-at-home/

- Using meal kit services isn't much better, with the average cost per serving nearly three times higher.

There is no way around it; if you want to save money on food, you need to cook more of your own food.

I am not saying you should never go out to a restaurant again. But, when you do go out to a restaurant, make it count.

- Going out to a restaurant to celebrate an occasion or to try a new experience has value.
- Grabbing lunch at a "big-box" restaurant or fast-food spot, because you were too lazy to pack a lunch to work, has no value.

How to save money on groceries

If step one to saving money on food is to buy and cook more of your food, step two is to spend less money at the grocery store.

Here are a few tips to reduce your monthly grocery bill:

1. Have a plan.
2. Focus on cost per serving.
3. Think of food as money.
4. Price hunting.

Have a plan

The executives at big food retail companies are not stupid people. They know that the more time people spend in a grocery store, the more money they are likely to spend.

That is why grocery stores are designed to make you cover as much distance in the store as possible. The more aisles you walk down, the more products you see, and the higher the possibility of you filling up your cart with stuff you don't need.

Something as simple as a written shopping list can help you from filling up your chart. You write down your shopping list before you enter the store; you buy what is on the list and nothing else.

To take this a step further, you might consider planning out all your meals for the week in advance. If you have a schedule that tells you what meals you are having on each day and all the ingredients required to make each meal, it becomes easier to stick to your grocery list.

Focus on the price per serving

If the way to save money on groceries is to minimize your cost per meal, you will need to minimize your cost per unit of food. Buying in bulk is one way to accomplish that goal.

When I look at food in the grocery store, I don't look at the sticker price; I **look at the cost per serving of each product**.

Let's consider two options for buying ground beef.

1. Half a pound of ground beef for $10
2. Three pounds of ground beef for $49

Many people would be scared of the $49 sticker price for the three pounds of ground beef and opt for the $10, half a pound serving. Let's look at those same options when measured in dollars per pound.

1. Half a pound of ground beef for $20 per pound
2. Three pounds of ground beef for $16.33 per pound.

Although the three-pound option costs $39 more, it is actually 18% cheaper on a per pound basis.

Focus on the price per serving, not the sticker price.

Think of food as money

A study by The Natural Resources Defense Council (NRDC) found that 40% of food that is produced ends up in a landfill and that the average American family throws out $2,000 worth of food every year[11].

Putting aside the moral implications of throwing that amount of food in the garbage when so many people are going hungry, it's also a huge waste of money.

---

[11] NRDC. (2012). Wasted: How America Is Losing Up to 40 Percent of Its Food from Farm to Fork to Landfill.

Next time you throw out produce because you let it rot, think to yourself, "I just threw $10 in the garbage".

If you think of food as money, you will be less likely to waste it.

Price hunting

Remember when people used to cut coupons out of the newspaper to save money on groceries? That still exists. Only now the process is done through apps.

First, every major grocery chain has its own app. While you are planning your meals for the week, you can easily hop on each store's app and see who has the cheapest ingredients for the meals you plan on making that week.

In addition to the grocery store-specific apps, there are lots of third-party websites where you can find tons of sales and coupons. The smart thing to do is find out what is on sale or what you can find a coupon for and make a meal plan around these items before you enter the grocery store.

It's not a good idea to buy something only because it's on sale or you have a coupon. Buying broccoli because you had a coupon is not a good use of money if you're not going to eat the broccoli. That's how we end up with food waste.

That is why making a meal plan is so important. Once you have a specific set of ingredients that you are going to buy, all you need to do is find it at the lowest price per serving. If you can find a coupon or a sale to bring the cost down further, that's great.

Chapter Recap

- The average person spends nearly 70% of their take-home pay on the big 3 expenses.

- Making any changes to your big three expenses has an opportunity cost. There is no free lunch. If you are going to spend less money on the big three expenses, it requires a sacrifice. Either a sacrifice in scaling back the lifestyle you are accustomed to or a sacrifice in dedicating more time to reduce your spending.

- Remember your "why" from chapter 1 when deciding what you are willing to sacrifice to improve your finances.

Chapter 4:

How Much Money Should You Have in an Emergency Fund?

An emergency fund means you have access to cash that you can use to pay your bills in the event of a financial emergency such as losing your job.

Most financial experts recommend having between three and six months' worth of living expenses in your emergency fund. The truth is that it depends on your personal circumstances. Some people are comfortable with a one-month emergency fund, while for others, it makes sense to have at least one year's worth of living expenses set aside.

Let's review all the factors you need to consider when building your emergency fund.

What expenses should an emergency fund cover?

The first step to building an emergency fund is to be crystal clear on what expenses you want your emergency fund to cover.

Many people think that an emergency fund should cover all their regular expenses. I look at an emergency fund as a way to guarantee I have enough money to cover all my **essential expenses**.

The following are the essential expenses that my emergency fund covers:

- Housing.

- Transportation.

- Groceries.

- Cell phone and internet.

- Minimum payments on debt.

- Medical bills and expenses.

- Child and childcare-related expenses.

- Any other expenses I absolutely can't cut.

I focus on essential expenses in my emergency fund because, if I am experiencing a genuine financial emergency, I will be forced to cut all non-essential expenses until the crisis is over.

Think about it this way: if you lost your job and your emergency fund was your only source of income, would you feel comfortable withdrawing from your emergency fund to take the family out to dinner and a movie?

I know you wouldn't.

Having lived through true financial emergencies in my life, my emergency fund has an obvious and specific purpose: keep a roof over my head and food on the table for as long as possible.

In certain circumstances, it makes sense to include "non-essential" expenses in your emergency fund. For example, if you have kids, would it make sense to add something like the cost of a Netflix subscription in your emergency fund?

It is certainly not "essential", but if shutting off the Netflix account without warning would cause conflict and stress at a time where you don't need either of those things, then you might want to include that in your emergency fund.

You need to be honest with yourself and identify which expenses you simply don't have the stomach to cut. Even if they are not essential, if you won't actually reduce these expenses, it's best to plan for that fact and include them in your emergency fund.

Just remember, the more expenses your emergency fund needs to cover, the more money you need to save.

You need to track your expenses

Good thing we already covered this in a previous chapter. Once you've tracked your average monthly expenses, identify which expenses you want to include when saving for your emergency fund and which expenses you would cut in the event of a job loss.

How many months' worth of living expenses should you have in your emergency fund?

After tracking several months' worth of expenses and figuring out how much you spend on average on the expenses you want your emergency fund to cover, the final thing you need to decide is how many months you would like your emergency fund to cover.

The typical advice is to have an emergency fund that can last for three to six months.

However, that number can change significantly depending on two factors:

1.   How secure your income is.

2.   Your personal preferences.

If you live in a two-income household with a high level of job security and where either partner's income could cover the necessary living expenses, you probably don't need an entire six-month emergency fund. Unless it simply makes you feel better to have six months' worth of expenses available in cash.

If having a large emergency fund will let you sleep better at night, then go for it. Personal finance is the art of balancing "the numbers" with your personal preferences.

On the other hand, if you have very little job security, you may want to consider a larger emergency fund.

Consider someone who is recently retired and gets the majority of their income from their investments. They may want to have one or even two years' worth of necessary living expenses in their emergency fund.

Should you invest your emergency fund?

Another question that people often ask is if it is okay to invest the money in their emergency fund in a risky asset like stocks.

You should never, under any circumstance, risk the money in your emergency fund.

Think about when most people need to rely on their emergency fund: when they have lost their job.

- When do a lot of people lose their job? During a recession.
- What happens to the stock market during a recession? It goes down.

If you've just lost your job and your emergency fund was reduced by 50% or more at the same time, you will be in a world of financial hurt.

I realize there is nothing fun or sexy about emergency funds, and that is by design. Think of your emergency fund as taking your financial medicine.

How much money should you be saving into your emergency fund each month?

If you're building a DIY savings plan, there are four factors that need to be considered:

1. How much you spend on your essential expenses each month.

2. How many months' worth of expenses you want in your emergency fund.

3. When you want your emergency fund to be fully funded.

4. How much you currently have saved in your emergency fund.

Let's say you track your expenses and determine that you spend $2,500 per month on necessary expenses. You also decide that you want a six-month emergency fund set up in five months and have $3,000 already saved.

- Your goal would be to have $15,000 ($2,500 X 6 months) saved in your emergency fund.

- Since you already have $3,000 saved, that means you need to save an additional $12,000.

- To fully fund your emergency fund in five months would mean you need to save $2,400 per month.

Chapter Recap

- Many experts recommend three to six months' worth of living expenses in an emergency fund. Make a list of all the expenses you would not be willing to cut, even in a financial emergency.

- Then track several months' worth of spending to determine how much you spend on these items.

- The final decision you need to make is how many months you would like your emergency fund to last, which will be mainly determined by how secure your income is and your personal preferences.

- An emergency fund should come before any financial goal, with the one exception of making the minimum payments on your debts.

Chapter 5:

Why Your Net Worth Can Be Misleading

Your net worth is equal to your assets minus debts and is a useful snapshot of the current state of your finances.

Your net worth allows you to compare your total assets to your total debts. Having a low or even negative net worth does not make you a financial failure.

Think of the recent college graduate who has no assets and a pile of student loan debt. Although the graduate will have a negative net worth, he has likely increased his or her ability to start building wealth.

Tracking your net worth over the years and decades can act as a useful measuring stick for how you are doing in your savings and debt repayment goals.

However, there are times where your net worth can trick you into thinking you are wealthier than you really are.

When your net worth can be misleading

The elephant in the room that needs to be addressed when talking about calculating your net worth is your house. If you own your home, the value of that home might be inflating your net worth.

If you're a homeowner, there is a decent chance that your home is the largest asset you own. That means it plays an outsized role in determining your net worth.

Your home equity is the difference between the value of your home and your mortgage. If you own a $500,000 house with a $400,000 mortgage, your home equity is $100,000, which increases your net worth by that same amount.

If you live in an area with a hot housing market, the value of your home may be inflating your net worth.

How home equity can become the most significant component of your net worth

Owning can be a great way to increase your net worth in the long run. Here is the general path to how home equity becomes the most significant component of many people's net worth.

- You use cheap debt (a mortgage) to buy a very expensive asset at a relatively young age.

- On day one of owning a home, your equity is equal to the down payment you used to buy the house.

- Over the years, the value of your home increases, and the amount of your mortgage gradually decreases. This begins to increase your home equity and your net worth steadily.

- Given all the expenses involved in owning a home, you don't have a lot of extra cash left over to save and invest in other assets. As a result, your home equity becomes the most significant component of your net worth.

Why you don't want your home equity to be the most significant component of your net worth

The problem with having too much of your net worth tied up in your home is that it can be challenging to access your home equity.

If you own a house worth $1 million and have paid off your mortgage, you are technically a millionaire, even if you don't have any other assets or savings. If you're nearing retirement age and you want to begin living off that $1 million net worth, you will quickly realize how impractical it is to have all your net worth tied up in an asset that you live in and have an emotional attachment to.

There are only three ways to access the equity in your home and use it to fund your lifestyle:

1. Sell your home and rent.

2. Sell your home and buy another home.

3. Take out a loan against your home.

All these options are less than ideal.

Selling your home and renting

The simplest way to access the equity in your home is to sell your house. While this solves the problem of how to access your home equity, it presents a new problem: you need to find somewhere to live.

One option would be to start renting. Selling your home to begin renting is a double edge sword.

- On the one hand, you can access the equity in your home and start spending the money.

- On the other hand, by paying rent, you just added a significant monthly expense. If you've had your mortgage paid off for many years, this will likely be a substantial increase in your cost of living.

This assumes that you are willing to sell your house in the first place. For many, a house is not only their largest asset but the place they raised their children and where they have countless memories. This is another reason you don't want the majority of your net worth tied up in your house.

Not only is it difficult to access the equity, but the emotional attachment can also prevent you from making "*cold, rational decisions*" like you would with any other asset.

Downsizing

Another way to potentially access some of the equity in your home is to sell your house and buy a smaller, less expensive home. This option allows you to retain ownership of an asset while accessing some of the cash tied up in your home.

If you sold your four-bedroom house for $500,000 and bought a 2-bedroom condo for $250,000, you could access up to $250,000 of the equity in your home minus transaction and closing costs involved in that transaction (which can be significant).

Downsizing is far from a slam dunk, and it is critical that the numbers line up, or it could end up being a disaster. You still need to use a significant amount of your home equity to buy the smaller home, which makes it inaccessible again.

In the example above, selling the home and buying the condo would mean you have $250,000 in cash and $250,000 in equity in the condo (minus closing costs). That means you only have $250,000 in cash to live off.

Condos also have condo fees, which are typically hundreds of dollars per month.

Like selling to rent, selling to downsize might be a non-starter if you are unwilling to leave your home.

Using debt to access your home equity

If you're unwilling to leave your home, the only way to access the equity in your home is to take out a loan against the value of your home, which typically means a mortgage.

Like with renting, taking out a mortgage against a paid-off home significantly increases your monthly cost of living, as you now have a mortgage payment.

If your home is your only asset, taking out a mortgage is extremely risky as you are using borrowed money to make the mortgage payment.

Calculating your accessible net worth

If you want to avoid the situation where the bulk of your net worth at retirement age is tied up in your home, you'll want to track what I call your "accessible net worth", which is your net worth excluding the value of your primary residence.

Compare your accessible net worth to your official net worth to gain a sense of how much your wealth is derived from your home.

- Start by calculating your net worth.
- Then simply subtract the value of the house (the asset) but leave the mortgage (the debt).
- The result is your accessible net worth.

For example, let's say your assets and debts were as follows:

Assets

- Home: $500,000
- Cash: $10,000

- Retirement accounts $125,000
- Other investments $85,000

    Total assets: $720,000

    Debts

- Mortgage: $250,000

    Net worth: $470,000

Here's how your accessible net worth would look:

Assets

- Cash: $10,000
- Retirement accounts $125,000
- Other investments $85,000

    Total accessible assets: $220,000

    Debts

- Mortgage: $250,000

    Accessible net worth: negative $30,000

Think of your accessible net worth as the level of wealth you could access if you decided to never sell your home.

Accessible net worth highlights our dependency on our primary residence

The above example showed how someone with a nearly quarter-million in net worth could have a negative accessible net worth. You might ask why we would not include the value of the home, but we would include the mortgage.

The reason is simple.

- As we have reviewed in detail, it is difficult to access the value of your home and convert it into cash.

- Your mortgage, on the other hand, is a liability that you must pay every month (or risk losing your home).

The point of calculating your accessible net worth

The point I want to drive home with the concept of accessible net worth is the importance of building a diverse base of assets that you can easily access. This is not a commentary on whether or not you should own a home or rent.

To provide yourself with the highest degree of financial flexibility, **it's crucial to have access to money and assets that are independent of the house you live in.**

If your accessible net worth is dramatically lower than your traditional net worth, that does not mean that you should sell your house. It simply means you might need to focus on contributing more to your retirement accounts.

Chapter Recap

- Owning a home is a great way to build wealth over the long run. Over time, as the value of your home increases and the balance on your mortgage increases, your net worth will increase.

- However, it's important to know that accessing the net worth in your home can be very difficult, especially if you have a strong emotional attachment to your home.

- For that reason, you don't want too much of your net worth tied up in your home.

- The concept of an accessible net worth helps you determine how much wealth you have access to if you choose never to sell your home.

- If you own your home, your accessible net worth is likely much lower than your traditional net worth.

- This is not intended to dissuade anyone from buying a house but to highlight the importance of diversifying your assets and investing in assets apart from your primary residence.

- Having a high net worth is not worth much if you can't use it to fund the lifestyle you want.

Chapter 6:

How To Increase Your Savings Rate

Tell me your savings rate, and I'll tell you where you'll be financially in five years.

Your savings rate is the most important number to monitor when pursuing financial independence because it's not your *total* wealth that matters; it's your wealth *relative* to your living expenses.

The higher your savings rate today, the more wealth you will have relative to your expenses in the future. No matter what anyone says, it doesn't matter how much wealth you have; it only matters how much wealth you have relative to your living expenses.

How to calculate your savings rate

We need to start by establishing a shared understanding of what your savings rate means. To do that, you'll need to know the difference between gross and take-home pay.

- **Gross pay**= The total amount you make before any taxes or deductions are considered.

- **Take-home pay**= The total amount you make per month after taxes or deductions. This is the amount that hits your checking account on payday.

Savings rate = (monthly savings ÷ take-home pay) X 100%. Say your monthly take-home pay is $10,000 and you save $5,000, your savings rate is 50%.

What should you consider "savings"?

Some people overthink their savings rate by only including money that is invested or other arbitrary rules. I have a much simpler definition of what constitutes savings:

I consider savings to be any use of money that will increase your net worth.

That includes the principal portion of any loan payment. Every dollar of principal paid increases your net worth by a dollar.

However, I do not include savings that are intended for future consumption.

For example, I have a savings account I use as a vacation fund. It's been accumulating a decent balance recently because I have not had the opportunity to travel. I don't consider it as savings because the purpose of this money is to be spent in the near term.

Now that we have a shared understanding of how to calculate your savings rate, let's get into the good stuff and talk about how to boost yours.

How to increase your savings rate

Remember, there are only two variables in the savings rate equation:

1. How much money you make.

2. How much money you save.

Therefore, there are only two actions you can take to increase your savings rate:

1. **Reduce your spending** while maintaining your current income.

2. **Increase your income** while maintaining your current spending.

Let's dig into each of these ideas a bit further.

Want to reduce your spending? Think houses, not lattes

One of the most tired takes on personal finance is that the key to saving more money is by cutting back on small purchases like lattes. Call me a radical thinker, but it seems to me **if you want to reduce your spending, you should look at the largest − not the smallest − line items on your budget.**

That means looking at the big 3 expenses:

1. Housing.

2. Transportation.

3. Food.

Luckily, we already dedicated an entire chapter of this book to the big 3 living expenses.

Cutting your living expenses is a great way to quickly increase your savings rate. If you can keep your savings rate low, it also means you need less total wealth to one day cover those living expenses and achieve financial freedom (more on that in part 2 of the book).

Once you have cut your expenses to the lowest amount you are comfortable with, the next step to obtaining an ultra-high savings rate is increasing your income.

A side hustle is an incredible way to increase your savings rate

One reason many people struggle to save money is that they have a tendency to spend based on their paycheck and only save if there is money left over after they bought everything they wanted.

There are ways people with one paycheck can increase their savings, like automating their savings and then spending what is left. However, it is much easier for most people from a psychological perspective to save money they earn from a side hustle or second job.

Since side hustle money is independent of your 9–5 paycheck, you may find it easier to look at that money as separate money and dedicate it to saving. That is exactly what I do with my side hustle money, which perfectly complements my 9–5 paycheck:

- I have a job that provides a nice paycheck, excellent benefits, and a defined benefit pension.

- My paycheck and benefits cover my retirement income (through the pension), any medical or dental expenses (through my benefits), and all my living expenses with a healthy amount left over to save and invest (through my paycheck).

- This allows me to save and invest every single penny I earn from my side hustle.

After three years, my take-home pay from my side hustle is roughly the same as my 9–5 paycheck. This has allowed me to achieve an ultra-high savings rate of more than 80%.

An 80% savings rate allows me to quickly build up more wealth relative to my living expenses.

In my opinion, a digital business with limited customer service is the best bet for someone looking to start a side hustle. It allows you to be completely flexible when you work, which is crucial if you hold down a traditional 9–5 job.

Start with baby steps

For many people reading this, the idea of achieving this kind of savings rate may not feel realistic. Boosting your savings rate is not something that happens overnight; it's a long-term process.

In 2010, I could barely pay my rent, let alone save and invest for the future. But over the years, as my income began gradually increasing and my debts melted away, I began to build more confidence.

So, how do you achieve an ultra-high savings rate?

One small step at a time.

Chapter Recap

- Your savings rate is the percentage of your take-home pay that you dedicate to long-term saving and investing or principal payments on your debt.

- The higher your savings rate today, the faster your wealth will grow relative to your living expenses.

- There are two ways to increase your savings rate: increasing your income while keeping your cost of living flat OR reducing your living expenses while keeping your income flat.

- A side hustle can allow you a separate income stream which may be easier to save rather than spend.

- Increasing your savings rate is a gradual process that requires you to remain focused on the task at hand.

Chapter 7:

Everything You Need to Know About Debt

Many people think that debt is evil. When you think of the millions of people who have declared bankruptcy and have spent the majority of their life living in debt, you can understand why people believe that debt is evil.

With one notable exception (more on that in a minute), debt is not evil. In fact, debt is not even bad. **The problem is how most people use debt**.

If you are struggling with debt, you are going to want to read this chapter in its entirety to learn the difference between good debt and bad debt, how people fall into debt and how to get out of debt.

What is debt?

Debt is simply a financial tool that allows you to buy something if you don't have enough money available to make the purchase using cash.

Debt is no more "evil" or "bad" than a physical tool like a hammer. It is the misuse of this financial tool that causes pain and suffering to so many people.

- If you use debt in the right way, it has the potential to increase your wealth and improve your life.

- If you use debt in the wrong way, it will take you down the path to financial misery.

Let me be clear on what I mean when I say, "If you use debt the right or wrong way." Four factors will determine if you are using debt properly:

1. The type of debt you are using.

2. The purpose of which you are using that debt.

3. How much debt you take on.

4. The interest rate and repayment terms of that debt.

Those four factors are what make the difference between good debt and bad debt.

Good debt vs. bad debt

To further clarify the difference between good debt and bad debt, let's review the eight types of debt and rank them from worst to best.

1. Payday loans

Remember when I said debt is not "evil"? I need to amend that statement because there is one type of debt that might actually be evil, and that is **payday loan**.

What are payday loans? **Payday loans are bridge loans to provide cash for people who have run out of money and need to pay bills before their next paycheck.**

That sounds pretty harmless. In fact, it sounds like it provides real value to the borrower. You might be wondering why payday loans are bad? The issue with payday loans is that they have the potential to hook borrowers into dependency and keep them coming back every month.

Think of it this way: if you can't afford to pay your bills this month, there is a decent chance you won't be able to pay your bills next month. This is especially true when you just added a new loan that needs to be paid off on top of your regular expenses.

Here are two stunning statistics about payday loans:

1. 80% of payday loan borrowers are repeat customers[12].

2. According to a report from the Centre for responsible investing, the typical Average Percent Rate (APR) on a payday loan ranges from 391% to 443%[13].

Payday loans can trap you in a vicious cycle of dependency on ultra-high interest debt. For that reason, payday loans are the worst type of debt and must be avoided.

---

[12] Singletary, M., Singletary, M., & Singletary, M. (2015, March 28). *Perspective | The vicious cycle of payday loans.* Washington Post. https://www.washingtonpost.com/business/get-there/the-vicious-cycle-of-payday-loans/2015/03/27/4ff7bec2-d3e1-11e4-ab77-9646eea6a4c7_story.html

[13] *Quantifying the Economic Cost of Predatory Payday Lending.* (2003, December). Center for responsible lending.

2. Credit cards

In contrast to payday loans, credit cards are not "bad". They are, however, the most mismanaged and abused type of debt in the world today. The average American owes $5,700 on their credit card[14]. If that does not sound like a lot of money, consider the fact that the average[15] APR for credit cards was over 16% in May 2020. It's not uncommon for credit card rates to be as high as 20% or even 30%.

You can't find an investment that can guarantee you a 16%-30% annual rate of return. It does not exist. If you carry a credit card balance, credit card companies are making more money off you than Warren Buffett or any investment manager could ever make in the stock market.

How to manage credit cards

Managing credit cards is simple. There is one golden rule to successfully managing credit cards: **always pay off your outstanding balance immediately after making a purchase.** If you do that, you will avoid all the pitfalls of credit cards and begin building up your credit score.

---

[14] Resendiz, J. (2021, March 22). *Average Credit Card Debt in America: 2021.* ValuePenguin. https://www.valuepenguin.com/average-credit-card-debt

[15] Dilworth, K. (2021, June 30). *Average credit card interest rates: June 30, 2021.* CreditCards.Com. https://www.creditcards.com/credit-card-news/rate-report/

This means you only use your credit card to buy something that you could have purchased using cash. To make this easier, most credit card companies offer a grace period where no interest is charged. Typically, this grace period is three weeks. If you pay your credit card balance within the grace period, you won't be charged interest.

Credit card cash advances

It's important to know that this three week grace period for credit cards does not apply to cash advances made on your card. A credit card cash advance is when you use your credit card at an ATM to withdraw cash.

There are three crucial facts you need to know about using your credit card to get a cash advance:

1. **Interest begins accruing immediately.** There is no grace period; you start racking up interest the second the ATM spits the money out.

2. **Cash advance interest rates are higher than standard credit card rates.** The average interest rate on cash advances is around 24%[16].

3. **You pay an additional administration fee.** To rub salt in the wound, credit card companies

---

[16] Staples, A. (2020, September 4). *Credit Card Cash Advance; What You Need To Know.* CreditCards.Com. https://www.creditcards.com/credit-card-news/what-is-cash-advance/

often charge an administration fee in addition to the interest you pay on cash advance. These fees might be a flat rate like $5 or $10, or it could be a percentage of the amount of the cash advance you are making.

How to read a credit card statement

If you have never reviewed your monthly credit card statement, you should because it contains a lot of useful information.

Let's review a sample credit card statement from an old credit card I had several years ago. Every month your credit card company should send you a statement that looks something like this:

Your monthly statement contains a lot of information and can feel intimidating. It's not as complicated as it looks, and specifically, we will be looking for the following information on a credit card statement:

- Name of the financial institution that issued you the credit card. If you have multiple credit cards with the same bank, you could sort them by the type of card. For example, the card in the sample image above is called an "Aventura Visa Infinite" card.

- You're also going to need to know the current balance on the card.

- The interest rate you pay on any outstanding balance.

- The minimum payment required.

- The due date of that minimum payment.

- Consequences of missing that minimum payment due date.

If we zoom in a little closer, we can easily find that information.

Your account at a glance

Previous balance		$415.59
Payments	$2,260.00	
Other credits	0.00	
Total credits		- $2,260.00
Purchases	2,129.93	
Cash advances	0.00	
Interest	0.00	
Fees	0.00	
Total charges		+ $2,129.93
New balance		= $285.52

Your minimum payment due

Current month's minimum payment	$10.00
Please pay this amount by Sep 08, 2015	

The first thing you'll likely notice is what's usually called a "summary of account activity" or, as my bank called it, "your account at a glance".

Let's go through this line by line to understand what we are reading.

- **Previous balance**: Balance on the credit card last month.

- **Payments**: Total amount of payments you have made since the last statement

- **Other credits**: Total of any other transactions that reduce your credit card balance, for example, returning an item and having it refunded on your card.

- **Total credits**: Payments + Other credits.

- **Purchases**: Total cost of all the things you purchased with your credit card since the last statement.

- **Cash advances**: Total of any cash you have borrowed from your credit card since the last statement.

- **Interest**: Any interest you have been charged from carrying a balance on your credit card.

- **Fees**: Any other fees charged to your account.

- **Total charges**= Purchases + Cash advances + Interest + Fees.

- New balance: This is how much you currently owe on your credit card and is equal to your **Previous balance + total charges – total credits.**

It's crucial that you carefully read your credit card account statement every month. It has vital information that you will need to manage your credit card.

Credit card reward points

If you follow the golden rule of managing a credit card, you will put yourself in a position to take advantage of one of the major perks of owning a credit card: **reward points**.

There are many different types of credit card reward programs, but the two most common are travel and cash-back rewards.

1. Travel reward programs allow you to collect points for each purchase you make using that card. These points can typically be redeemed for flights, hotels, and vacation packages.

2. Cashback reward programs provide a cash rebate for each purchase you make with that card. These rebates are typically around 1%-2% of the value of purchases made on the card. Many rebate programs provide different cashback rates for various purchases. For example, some cards give a higher percentage of cashback at grocery stores and gas stations.

In addition to points and cashback, credit card reward programs also provide additional perks to the cardholder. For example, my travel reward card gives me free insurance coverage on rental cars.

A word of caution about credit card reward programs: these reward programs incentivize you to spend money. The more money you spend, the *more points you get.* **You should never spend money simply to collect credit card points.**

That might sound obvious, but you would be amazed how many people justify purchases they don't need to make because "I get points". Credit card companies are not stupid. They know that people respond to incentives. Use the reward programs, but don't let them use you.

Another word of caution on credit cards that offer a reward program: don't get fooled into paying a high annual fee for the privilege of collecting points.

Often, credit cards that have a reward program offer two different versions of the same credit card.

1. A version of the card with a less generous reward system with a small or even no annual fee.

2. A version of the card with a more generous rewards system with a higher annual fee.

Let me repeat it, credit card companies are not stupid. They know that many people will take the card with a high annual fee for the sole purpose of collecting more points.

Depending on how much money you spend per year, it is possible that the more generous rewards program could justify the higher annual fee. Still, for most people, it's best to stay away for a straightforward reason. **The high fee credit card incentivizes you to spend more money.**

Think about two versions of a cash back rewards card:

- Card 1: Offers 1% cash back and has no annual fee.
- Card 2: Offers 2% cash back and has a $120 annual fee.

You would need to spend $12,000 per year or $1,000 per month just to break even on card 2. This provides an incentive to spend at least $1,000 per month to justify the choice to go with the high-fee credit card. You may not even be aware that this is happening, but somewhere in your subconscious is a voice telling you to get the points.

When in doubt, choose the credit card with no annual fee.

While credit cards themselves are not evil, mismanaging a credit card can have devastating consequences on your finances. As long as you always pay off your balance immediately and opt for a card with a low or no annual fee, a credit card can be a valuable financial tool.

3. Personal loans and lines of credit

Unsecured personal loans and lines of credit are other forms of debt that people often abuse.

The term "unsecured" refers to the fact that there is no collateral attached to these loans. A mortgage is a "secured" loan, meaning the loan is secured against your home. If you don't pay your mortgage, the bank can take your home.

This is not the case for unsecured loans and lines of credit, which is why they have a higher interest rate than a mortgage or other secured loans. The bank takes on more risk with an unsecured loan or line of credit, so they charge a higher interest rate to compensate themselves for taking that risk.

You might be wondering what the difference between a loan and a line of credit is?

A personal loan is a lump sum of cash. It is useful for financing a large, one-time purchase like a car. It can also be used as a way to consolidate higher-interest debt like credit cards. Payments on a loan typically begin as soon as you receive the money.

A personal line of credit is a financial instrument where you are granted the right but not the obligation to borrow money up to a maximum amount. For example, if you are approved for a $10,000 line of credit, you can choose to borrow between $0 and $10,000. You only pay interest on the outstanding balance of your line of credit.

Personal loans and lines of credit can be useful if you need to consolidate higher interest rate debt like credit cards and payday loans into a single monthly payment with a lower interest rate.

On the other hand, if you use personal loans or lines of credit to fuel consumption like buying a new TV or going on a vacation you can't afford, they can get you into financial hot water.

4. Car loans

I am not a big fan of cars. They are most people's second-largest expense in life and for most people, where they waste the most money.

I am also no fan of car loans because they trick people into buying a more expensive car than they need. Just because someone will lend you $30,000 to buy a car does not mean you can afford or need to buy a $30,000 car.

Sadly, this is precisely how many people make their decision on what car to buy. They buy the most expensive car for which someone will lend them the money to buy. Borrowing money and paying interest to buy something that will one day be worthless is not a smart financial move.

That is why **The average car loan payment for a new car is over $563 per month**[17]. Take a moment and compare that number to the amount you save for retirement each month. If you spend more money on your car payment than your retirement savings, you need to get your financial priorities straight.

---

[17] *Average Car Payment | Loan Statistics 2021.* (2021). LendingTree. https://www.lendingtree.com/auto/debt-statistics/#:%7E:text=Key%20facts%20about%20auto%20loans,5%25%20of%20American%20consumer%20debt.

Rather than going further into debt to buy a "cool" car, why not buy the crappiest (and safest) car you find and redirect the savings toward our financial goals?

5. Loans from family and friends

Not all debt comes from credit card companies or banks. Oftentimes, people borrow money from their friends and family. It's difficult to rank these types of loans because they have the highest variance in outcomes.

Borrowing money from close friends and family can work out great if you repay the loan in the agreed-upon timeframe. This could be a lifesaver if you need cash but can't get a loan from a bank. Depending upon your relationship with the person lending you money, you might get a lower rate than the bank would charge.

However, there are a lot of risks involved in borrowing money from people you know, and it goes beyond financial risk. You risk losing your relationship with that person.

Lending money to a family member was the worst decision I ever made. Not only did I lose a lot of money, but things got so ugly that I lost my relationship with that family member. We never reconciled and will never have the opportunity to do so.

There are some things in life more valuable than money, and relationships with the right people are one of those things. Never borrow money from friends or family unless you are willing to potentially sacrifice your relationship with that person.

6. Student loans

We are now officially out of "consumer loans", which is when you take on debt to buy "stuff", and now moving into "investment loans".

Student debt is a tricky issue. On the one hand, it has never been more expensive to get a college education. That is why 54% of college graduates have student debt, and the average student loan is $37,584[18].

On the other hand, college graduates have the lowest levels of unemployment and earn more money than people who did not graduate from college.

Here are some stats from the Social Security Administration[19] about the impact of education on lifetime earning potential.

- Men with bachelor's degrees earn $900,000 more lifetime earnings than male high school graduates.

- Women with bachelor's degrees earn $630,000 more than female high school graduates.

[18] Student Loan Debt: 2020 Statistics and Outlook. (2020). Investopedia. https://www.investopedia.com/student-loan-debt-2019-statistics-and-outlook-4772007

[19] *Research Summary: Education and Lifetime Earnings*. (2015). U.S Social Security Website. https://www.ssa.gov/policy/docs/research-summaries/education-earnings.html

The numbers are even more lopsided for those who complete graduate school.

- Men with graduate degrees earn $1.5 million more lifetime earnings than male high school graduates.
- Women with graduate degrees earn $1.1 million more lifetime earnings than female high school graduates.

Education is an investment in yourself. I took on $50,000 in debt to complete my master's degree, and it was one of the best decisions I ever made. It increased my income substantially and allowed me to easily get out of debt and quickly begin building wealth.

Whether or not student loans end up being good debt or bad debt depends entirely on you. If you don't over-extend yourself and leverage your education into a high-paying career, it can be a great decision.

If you flunk out of school or never pursue a career related to the education you received, then student loans are a waste of money, and going to college was a waste of time.

Anytime you invest in yourself, the outcome will be entirely dependent upon what you do.

7. Mortgages

In many circumstances, owning a home can be an excellent financial decision. A mortgage allows you to buy an asset worth hundreds of thousands of dollars without having the money upfront.

As a form of debt, mortgages are as good as you will get.

- The interest rate for mortgages is lower than any other type of debt you will find.
- You have longer to repay the debt (up to 30 years) than any other type of debt you will find.

That being said, don't go overboard and buy a bigger house than you need. A bigger house means a bigger mortgage, which means higher monthly payments. If you have a four-bedroom house but only use one bedroom, you are paying interest on three rooms you don't use.

A bigger house also means higher property taxes, utilities, and maintenance costs. In the same way that a car loan can trick someone into thinking they can afford a nicer car, a mortgage tricks many people into thinking they can afford a bigger house.

Buying a home and taking on a mortgage is one of the most important financial decisions you are likely to make. You need to be smart about it. Buy the least amount of house you are comfortable living in and minimize the size of your mortgage.

8. Loans to buy income-producing assets

The best kind of loan is one which is used to buy investments that will increase in value and pay you income along the way.

Examples of income-producing assets:

- Real estate.
- Stocks.
- Businesses.

Borrowing money to invest is called leverage. Leverage can increase your investment returns and your net worth. Still, it also increases your level of risk and, if misused (or if you simply have bad luck) can have disastrous financial consequences.

Using leverage to invest in real estate

There are two simple reasons many real estate investors have a high net worth:

1. They buy assets using other people's money.
2. They get other people to pay their debts for them.

Real estate investors can buy properties worth hundreds of thousands of dollars using other people's money. Most often, this means taking out a mortgage to buy a property.

Here is an example that illustrates the power of leverage in real estate investing.

Let's say you buy a house worth $100,000 and use $20,000 of your own money and borrow $80,000 in the form of a mortgage. After one year, the price of that home has increased to $105,000. What is your return on investment?

Some people might say 5% ($5,000/$100,000), which feels right but is wrong. Remember, you only put down $20,000 and have a $5,000 return, which means you had a 25% return on your money ($5,000/$20,000). This is an oversimplification and ignores all the costs associated with owning real estate but illustrates the power of leverage in real estate.

The other added benefit of using leverage to invest in real estate is that if you have made a smart investment, your tenants will pay your mortgage for you. A smart real estate investment will be "Cash flow positive" from day one, meaning you should be collecting enough rent to pay for the mortgage you used to buy the property and all the other expenses associated with the property like maintenance, insurance, and taxes.

Using leverage to invest in the stock market

There are three ways to use leverage to invest in the stock market:

1. Using what is called "margin".

2. Taking out a personal loan or line of credit.

3. Using the equity in your home.

Margin is money that is borrowed from an investment brokerage firm used to purchase an investment. The term margin is used because it is the difference (aka the margin) between the total value of your investments and the amount you borrowed from the brokerage. Any assets held inside your investment account are used as collateral for the loan.

Using margin to invest is very risky and is something that most people should never engage in. In addition to the interest you need to pay on the loan, if the value of your investments drops too much, you could be subject to what is called a "margin call", where the broker calls the loan and demands you repay it.

While it is useful to know what margin is for educational purposes, it is not something I would ever recommend.

Another option to use leverage to invest in stocks would be to use a personal loan or line of credit. This is straightforward; you use the loan to invest in the stock market and deduct the interest against your taxable income. The problem is that it might be more challenging to get approved for a loan to invest in stocks, and you would likely have a relatively high interest rate.

Finally, if you are a homeowner and you have enough equity in your home, you might be able to borrow against the value of your home to invest.

There are two possible ways to do this.

1. Refinancing your mortgage.

2. Taking out a Home Equity Lines of Credit (HELOC).

You already know what a mortgage is. It's a loan against your home, which often has a fixed interest rate, pre-determined payments, and amortization schedule (when you are set to pay the mortgage off).

You may not be familiar with HELOCs, which is a line of credit that is secured against the value of your home. HELOCs typically have lower interest rates than unsecured lines of credit. The reason for this is because you are securing the line of credit against your home, meaning if you default on the loan, you could potentially lose your home.

For the vast majority of people reading this, it's not worth the risk to use leverage to invest in the stock market. This is especially true if you are putting your home on the line. The potential benefits seldom outweigh the potential downside.

Taking out a loan to start a business

One of the most critical functions that banks play in society is lending money to entrepreneurs to start new businesses. The more people that start a business, the more wealth and jobs are created.

Owning a business and especially starting a brand-new business is the definition of "high-risk, high-reward". It's a well-known fact that the majority of businesses fail. This makes them a very risky proposition. On the other hand, owning a profitable business is one of the fastest ways to generate wealth.

Most of the wealthiest people in the world built their fortunes by owning profitable businesses.

However, for many entrepreneurs, the motivation to start a business is not strictly financial. They may be pursuing a particular passion or want to enjoy the flexibility that owning a business provides. If a business is profitable, the owner can pay employees to run the business for them.

Any debt used to invest, whether it be in real estate, the stock market, or to start a business, is the best type of debt for two reasons:

1. The interest on that debt is typically tax-deductible.

2. The debt is attached to an asset that produces income, unlike consumer debt which is attached "to stuff" that has no financial value and generates no income.

That being said, using debt to invest or start a business still involves a high degree of risk. If you overextend yourself or simply have bad luck, you could lose the asset you invested in and be stuck with the loan. That could have disastrous results.

Anyone considering using debt to invest should only do so after a great deal of planning. Preferably that planning should be done with a financial planner.

The importance of a good credit score

Your credit score has a massive impact on your relationship with debt. The better your credit score, the more likely you are to get approved for a loan, and the lower the interest rate on that loan will be.

In the U.S, credit scores range from 300–850, while in Canada, they range from 300–900. Here is what is considered a good and bad credit score.

- 300–649 is considered a "bad" credit score.

- 650–699 is considered a "fair" credit score.

- 700–749 is considered a "good" credit score.

- 750+ is considered an "excellent" credit score.

Let's consider the example of three people who have the same job, make the same income but have different credit scores who are all applying for a mortgage.

1. James has a credit score of 450, which is considered to be bad.

2. Jill has a credit score of 678, which is considered to be good.

3. John has a credit score of 808, which is considered to be excellent.

They all apply for a mortgage with the same bank.

- James is declined and unable to buy the home of his dreams.

- Jill is approved for a $240,000 mortgage, a 3.8% interest rate.

- John is approved for a $240,000 mortgage at a 2.5% interest rate.

Jill is clearly in a better position than James. The difference between a fair credit score and a bad credit score could be the difference between getting approved for a loan or not.

But how much better off is John compared to Jill? How much will he save on interest due to his excellent credit score?

- John will pay $101,384 in interest over the next 30-years.

- Jill will pay $162,587 in interest over the same time frame.

In this example, the difference between an excellent and fair credit score is $61,203. That is additional money that John could be using to either invest or make additional principal payments against his mortgage, saving him even more in interest and having his mortgage paid off sooner.

How to improve your credit score

Clearly, having an excellent credit score should be everyone's goal. But what if your credit score is terrible right now? How does someone improve their credit score?

Your credit score is primarily determined by the following factors:

1. Your history of paying bills on time.

2. How far back your credit history goes.

3. The amount of debt you are currently carrying.

4. How much of your credit limits you are currently using.

5. The mix of credit accounts on your file.

6. The number of credit inquiries/applications you have made.

So, if you want to begin improving your credit score, the first step is to simply pay all your bills, including your loan payments, on time. Make a promise to never be late on a bill payment again. This is both the most critical factor in improving your credit score in the long run and the action that is most in your control.

The length of your credit history also plays a role. If you don't have any history of credit use, applying for a credit card (that you will use responsibly) might be an excellent way to establish a credit history.

Another important factor impacting your credit score is what is called your "utilization ratio". This is a measure of how much of your available credit you are currently using.

Let's say you have a credit card and a line of credit.

- The credit card has a $10,000 limit, and you have a $7,000 balance.
- The line of credit has a $50,000 limit, and you have a $10,000 balance.
- That makes for a total of $60,000 in available credit and a combined balance of $17,000

That works out to a 28.3% utilization ratio. A low utilization ratio has a positive impact on your credit score.

To improve your utilization ratio, you can do two things:

1. Begin paying off debt.
2. When you pay off debt with a revolving balance, don't close the account.

In the above example, if you could pay off the balance on your credit card and your line of credit, but you did not close either account, it would bring your utilization rate down to 0%. You would have a total of $60,000 available to borrow, and you aren't using any of it. That shows lenders that you know how to manage credit responsibly.

You also want to make sure that you aren't applying for too many credit products. If you get denied a loan due to low credit, the worst thing you can do is turn around and make five more applications at different banks. The more credit inquiries (loan applications) you make, the worst it will be for your credit score.

You shouldn't be afraid to apply for credit when you need it but be careful not to make too many applications in a short period.

How to get out of debt

Now for the part that anyone living in debt has been waiting for, let's discuss how to pay off that debt. Two proven strategies will help you pay off debt fast:

- The snowball method.
- The avalanche method.

What is the snowball method?

The snowball method is a debt repayment strategy in which you focus on paying off your debt with the smallest outstanding balance. It's a four-step process.

- Step 1: List your debts from smallest to largest.
- Step 2: Make minimum payments on all your debts except the smallest.
- Step 3: Pay as much as possible on your smallest debt.
- Step 4: Repeat until each debt is paid in full.

Why people love the snowball method

The snowball method is the most popular debt repayment strategy because it leans into a simple truth about personal finance; habits and actions are more important than technical knowledge.

The psychology behind the snowball method is that paying your loan with the smallest balance first enables you to get your first loan paid off as quickly as possible. Once you pay off that first loan, you gain confidence and begin to believe that you can pay the rest of your debts. This provides you energy and gets you excited to keep going.

I like the snowball method because it gives people hope. Many people believe that their current circumstances are "how it will always be". Having an early win and seeing a loan completely paid off can begin to change someone's belief about what is possible for them to accomplish.

What is the avalanche method?

The avalanche method is a debt repayment strategy in which you focus on paying off the loan with the highest interest rate first.

Here are the four steps to paying off your debts using the avalanche method:

- Step 1: List all your debts from the highest interest rate to the lowest interest rate.
- Step 2: Make minimum payments on all your debts except the debt with the highest interest rate.
- Step 3: Pay as much as possible on your debt with the highest interest rate.
- Step 4: Repeat until each debt is paid in full.

While the snowball method is about psychology, the avalanche method is about efficiency.

Why the avalanche method is effective

If the psychological aspects of paying off debt aren't a concern for you, and you don't need to have that feeling of a quick win, the avalanche method might be a good fit for you.

The avalanche method will allow you to pay off your debt as quickly as possible while paying the least amount of interest.

Snowball vs. Avalanche methods: A detailed breakdown

I'll use a hypothetical example to demonstrate precisely how you can use the snowball or the avalanche method to pay off debt.

Let's pretend you have the following debts.

- Credit card 1: $20,000 balance at a 22% interest rate.
- Credit card 2: $6,200 balance at a 16% interest rate.
- Credit card 3: $7,600 balance at a 17% interest rate.
- Student loan: $44,000 and 8% interest rate
- Line of credit: $3,500 balance and 7% interest rate

  Total debt: $81,300

  Your goal: Pay off all debts in six years.

How to pay off $81,300 in six years using the snowball & avalanche methods

The first step to paying off your debts, whether you use the snowball method or the avalanche method, is to calculate your minimum monthly payment on each loan.

After reviewing your monthly statement for each loan, you found the following minimum payments:

- Credit card 1: $200/month.
- Credit card 2: $62/month.
- Credit card 3: $76/month.
- Student loan: $350/month.
- Line of credit: $99/month.

Total minimum monthly payments: $787/month

How to use the snowball method

The order in which you would pay off these debts using the snowball method is as follows:

1. Line of credit
2. Credit card 2
3. Credit card 3
4. Credit card 1
5. Student loan.

If your goal is to pay all your debts off in six years, you will need to contribute $1,587 per month toward your debt. Initially, $787 will go toward minimum payments and $800 toward additional principal payments on the line of credit.

- After month four, the line of credit will be paid off. Then you will take the $99 minimum payment and the $800 of additional principal payments and use that money to pay an additional $899 toward credit card 2 while maintaining minimum payments on your other debts.

- After month 11, credit card 2 will be paid off. Then you will take the $62 minimum payment and the $899 of additional principal payments and use that money to pay an additional $961 toward credit card 3.

- After month 20, credit card 3 will be paid off. Then you will take the $76 minimum payment and the $961 of additional principal payments and use that money to pay an additional $1,037 toward credit card 1.

- After month 43, credit card 1 will be paid off. Then you will take the $200 minimum payment and the $1,037 of additional principal payments and use that money to pay an additional $1,237 toward the student loan.

- After 72 months (six years), the student loan will be paid off, and you will be debt-free.

During the six years, you would have paid $32,191 in interest using the snowball method.

Here is the summary of this:

Order in which each loan gets paid off	Original balance of each loan	total amount paid in interest on each loan during the six years	Number of months until each loan is paid off
Line of credit	$ 3,500.0	$ 50.8	4
Credit card 2	$ 6,200.0	$ 663.3	11
Credit card 3	$ 7,600.0	$ 1,718.4	20
Credit card 1	$20,000.0	$ 13,353.8	43
Student loan	$44,000.0	$ 16,405.0	72

How to use the avalanche method

The order in which you would pay off these debts using the avalanche method is as follows:

1. Credit card 1
2. Credit card 3
3. Credit card 2.
4. Student loan.
5. Line of credit

If your goal is to pay all your debts off in six years, you will need to contribute $1,562 per month toward your debt. Initially, $787 will go toward minimum payments and $775 toward additional principal payments on credit card 1.

- After month 26, credit card 1 will be paid off. Then you will take the $200 minimum payment and the

$775 of additional principal payments and use that money to pay an additional $975 toward credit card 3 while maintaining minimum payments on your other debts.

- After month 35, credit card 3 will be paid off. Then you will take the $76 minimum payment and the $975 of additional principal payments and use that money to pay an additional $1,051 toward credit card 2.

- After month 40, the line of credit will be paid off. Even though you had not yet made any additional payments on the line of credit, 40 months' worth of minimum payments were enough to clear that debt. So, you take the $99 minimum payment that was going toward the line of credit and apply that to credit card 2. At this point, you are paying $1,230 toward credit card 2.

- After month 42, credit card 2 will be paid off. Then you will take the $62 minimum payment and the $1,231 of additional principal payments and use that money to pay an additional $1,293 toward the student loan.

- After 72 months (six years), the student loan will be paid off, and you will be debt-free.

During the six years, you would have paid $28,791 in interest using the avalanche method.

This can be summarized in this table:

Order in which each loan gets paid off	Original balance of each loan	total amount paid in interest on each loan during the six years	Number of months until each loan is paid off
Credit card 1	$ 20,000.0	$ 5,316.2	26
Credit card 3	$ 7,600.0	$ 3,563.4	35
Credit card 2	$ 6,200.0	$ 3,424.9	42
Student loan	$44,000.0	$ 16,055.5	71
Line of credit	$ 3,500.0	$ 431.2	40

So, which is better: the snowball or the avalanche method?

- Both the snowball method and the avalanche method would have you debt-free in six years.

- If you used the avalanche method, you would save $3,400 in interest payments.

- If you used the snowball method, your first loan would be paid off two years sooner than the avalanche method.

If your measuring stick is getting debt-free in the most efficient way possible, the avalanche is the better strategy.

If you need to get a "quick win", pay off your first loan and keep going, then the snowball method will work best for you.

Which method you choose is not very important. What matters is that you stick with whatever strategy you pick and see it through to the end.

Chapter Recap

- As we have covered, debt is not evil. It is simply a financial tool.

- It is our mismanagement of that tool that causes so much pain and suffering.

- Not all debt is created equal.

- Taking on debt simply means you wanted to buy something you don't have the cash for today.

- Debt used to fuel consumption will lead to financial pain.

- Debt used to fuel investment either in yourself or in assets that produce income has the potential (but no guarantee) to help you build wealth.

- Your credit score is incredibly important and could be the difference between being approved for a loan or not.

- The most important step you can take toward improving your credit score is to pay all your bills, especially your debt payments, on time.

- There are two proven strategies to pay off debt: the snowball and avalanche methods.

- The snowball method will allow you to get an early win by paying off your first loan quickly.

- The avalanche method will minimize the interest you pay on your journey to becoming debt-free.

Chapter 8:

A Beginners Guide To DIY Retirement Planning

There's a dirty secret about retirement planning: It's a bunch of guesswork.

To accurately project how much money you'll need in retirement, you would need to know future investment returns and inflation, how your spending habits will change as you age, and when you will die. All of these critical variables are unknowable.

If you want the very best guess for how much you'll need in retirement, go to a financial planner. Specifically, go to a good financial planner who will run Monte Carlo simulations to determine the probability (best guess) of a successful retirement.

If you don't have the money to shell out to a quality financial planner, this chapter is for you.

We are going to cover the basic points you need to think about to build a DIY retirement plan. I want to stress that this is far from an exhaustive list of everything you need to know; it is very much a "beginner's guide." That means this should be the beginning, not the end, of your retirement planning research. A retirement plan is a living document; you need to constantly update and review it as your life changes.

With those caveats out of the way, let's get down to business.

What happens if you don't save for retirement?

If you have nothing saved by the time you reach retirement age, one of two scenarios will play out.

1. You work until you die.

2. You become dependent upon your children or the government to take care of you.

When working until you die is the best-case scenario, you know you are dealing with some terrible options.

I've heard some people say that they wouldn't mind working forever. They love their job and don't see themselves ever retiring, so saving is not a priority.

Here is the problem with that kind of thinking. It's easy to say you don't mind working forever when you are young and healthy. I am 33 years old, and I love what I do, and I would keep doing it forever if I could remain a healthy 33-year-old forever.

But I can't.

One day I'll get old, and my health will begin to fail. Working may be a lot less fun when it hurts to get out of bed in the morning. I have to be realistic and come to terms with the fact that there may come a day where I don't want to do any work at all.

When I think of how much my goals and dreams have changed between the age of 22–32, I can't imagine how much they will change by the time I am 72. It's not fair for my 32-year-old self to write checks that my 72-year-old self can't cash.

For the sake of argument, let's assume that even when I am 72 that I don't mind continuing to work. That decision may not be up to me. The future state of the economy or my health may prevent me from working.

If I've reached retirement age with very little savings and cannot work, what would become of me? I would have to rely on my family and the government to support me. The thought of being that type of burden stresses me out.

That is why it's crucial to save for retirement. If nothing else, at least provide yourself the option to retire by a certain age and live financially independently.

Saving for retirement and having more money than you need is a much better outcome than not saving for retirement and not having enough money.

How to figure out how much you need to save for retirement

Figuring out how much you should be saving for retirement is a four-step process.

Step 1: Decide how much income you will need in retirement.

Step 2: Determine how much money you need to have saved on the day you retire to generate your retirement income.

Step 3: Calculate how much you need to start saving right now.

Step 4: Ensure your success by automating your savings.

How much income do you need in retirement?

Most financial professionals recommend that you aim to replace 70% of your annual pre-retirement income in retirement. To be clear, there is nothing scientific about this number; it's nothing more than a generally agreed-upon number that could work for most people.

If you wanted to replace 70% of a $100,000 pre-retirement income, your goal would be to generate $70,000 per year in retirement.

The technical term for how much of your pre-retirement income you generate in retirement is referred to as a "replacement ratio."

Replacement ratio= Retirement income ÷ pre-retirement income

Retirement income can come from any combination of your personal savings, workplace and government pensions, and income from rental properties or any other consistent form of income you can depend on during your retirement.

Is 70% of your income enough to fund your retirement?

The goal of replacing 70% of your pre-retirement income is a rule of thumb.

Like all rules of thumb, it is severely limited and does not take any of the specifics of your life into account.

The 70% replacement ratio should be the starting point, not the endpoint when creating a goal for how much income you need in retirement. Depending on which of your living expenses increase and decrease during retirement a 70% of your pre-retirement income may be too much or not enough money to fund your desired lifestyle in retirement.

The critical thing to remember is that your income replacement ratio directly affects how much you need to save for retirement. The more income you want to replace, the more you need to save for retirement.

If you can replace 70% of your income in retirement, you will be in a better position than most people. However, if you want a retirement income customized to your life (who wouldn't?), you need to think about what you'll be spending money on in retirement.

What costs will decrease when I retire?

Many costs typically decrease or go away entirely in retirement. The three most significant expenses that may decrease in retirement are:

1. Saving for retirement.

2. Childcare costs.

3. Housing costs.

Saving for retirement

Once you retire, you no longer need to save for retirement. That might sound obvious to the point of being silly. However, it plays a massive role in how much cash you need each month in retirement.

Ironically, the more you save during your working years, the smaller your income replacement needs to be during retirement. That is because there is an inverse relationship between your saving rate and your income replacement ratio. If you were saving 20% of your income during your working years, that is 20% of your income that does not need to be replaced during retirement.

What percentage of your income you save for retirement is something that you need to factor in when deciding on your retirement income replacement ratio.

This illustrates how saving early and often makes your life easier.

I should make clear this is referring specifically to your retirement savings. You'll still need to save and budget for specific purposes like vacations or an emergency fund during retirement.

Childcare costs

It's no secret that having children is expensive. How expensive is it to raise a child these days? The USDA breaks down the annual cost of raising a child as follows[20].

- Age 0–2: $12,680
- Age 3–5: $12,730
- Age 9+: $13,180
- Age 15–17: $13,900

If you currently have two kids aged 5 and 9, you might be spending around $26,000 per year on child-related expenses. If that seems like a lot, remember these are averages, and that includes all costs of raising a child, from childcare to extra groceries to higher utility bills. All those costs add up quicker than you might think.

The good news? That $26,000 per year that you will not need to spend in retirement. This plays a massive role in your income replacement ratio.

---

[20] *Expenditures on Children by Families, 2015* (Miscellaneous Report No. 1528–2015). (2017, January). United States Department of Agriculture.

Of course, this assumes,

A.) you have kids and

B.) your kids are grown up and financially independent from you by the time you retire.

If you have grandkids that you want to spoil, you will want to factor that into your retirement budget and the amount of annual income you'll need.

Mortgage payment

If your mortgage is fully paid off by the time you retire, your housing costs will drop by the amount of your mortgage. You'll still have to pay for property taxes and maintenance, which both tend to be around 1% of the value of your house per year.

If you retire with no mortgage and a house worth $500,000, you would still need to budget for at least $10,000 per year plus your heating and utility costs.

If you choose to sell your house when you retire, that decision will impact your retirement lifestyle in two ways.

1. Adding that lump sum of money to your retirement savings will allow you to increase your expected income in retirement.

2. If you choose to rent or take out another mortgage, your housing expenses will increase.

Whether or not selling your home in retirement is a good financial decision will depend on whether the lump sum from selling your home will be large enough to cover any additional housing costs in retirement.

Geographical arbitrage

Geographical arbitrage is when you move from an area with a high cost of living to a low cost of living. This allows you to enjoy the same quality of life you currently enjoy on a smaller income.

If you lived and worked in New York City your whole life and then, in retirement, decided you wanted to live in a small beachside community in Mexico, your cost of living in retirement would only be a fraction of what it was during your working years. The lower your cost of living in retirement, the less of your pre-retirement income you need to replace in retirement.

Currently, my wife and I live outside Toronto, one of Canada's highest cost of living areas. When we retire, we plan to move to Nova Scotia, where I am from originally. If we sold the house we live in right now, we could buy a few acres of oceanfront property in Nova Scotia and still have several hundred thousand dollars left over.

If appropriately done, geographical arbitrage can have the dual benefits of increasing your current standard of living while at the same time reducing your cost of living and therefore reducing how much you need to save for retirement.

Geographical arbitrage is not something that you need to do. If you are happy living where you are, that is great. However, if you plan to move to a new city or country when you retire, you will need to consider how your cost of living will change as that will decrease or increase the amount of your pre-retirement income you must replace to fund your lifestyle.

What costs will increase during retirement?

Three costs generally increase during retirement.

1. Healthcare

2. Travel

3. Social costs

Healthcare

Healthcare is likely the most significant increased expense for retirees, especially in the U.S. According to a report from Fidelity, the average married couple retiring at 65 in the U.S will need to plan on spending $285,000 on healthcare-related costs in retirement[21]

Healthcare is a significant issue you will need to contend with in retirement, and you must consider health care

---

[21] Fidelity. (2019, April). *2019 Retiree Health Care Cost Estimate*. https://s2.q4cdn.com/997146844/files/doc_news/archive/b6f07a26-3aa9-4a98-af00-b1b783cfd552.pdf

costs when planning how much annual income you will need in retirement.

Travel

Travel is the most obvious expense that increases in retirement. When people have nothing but free time, they spend more money on travel. The more you value travel, the more this cost will increase in retirement.

Travel is a tricky issue because, for some people, this could be their most significant retirement expense, and for others, it may not change at all. You will want to think about how often you plan on traveling and what that will do to your cost of living in retirement.

Eating out and other social costs

When do you spend most of your money during your working years? For most people, the answer is on weekends and vacations. When we have time to catch up with friends and family, we are more likely to go out to dinner, for drinks, or to other social events.

You need to ask yourself if every day was a Saturday, how would your social life change, and how much would that cost? Because guess what?

In retirement, every day is a Saturday.

Emergency fund

It's a smart idea for you to increase the size of your emergency fund in retirement. This is especially true if your retirement income is largely dependent upon investment returns, which can be very volatile.

If the bulk of your retirement income comes from investments and the value of your investments and the income they produce drops significantly, that could jeopardize your retirement (more on that soon.)

However, if you had a big pile of cash sitting on the side lines, you could draw down on that cash while you wait for your investments to recover.

There is no magic number to determine how much money you should hold in cash during retirement. It will depend largely on your retirement income sources, level of risk in your investments, and personal preferences. If you were comfortable with a 3–6-month emergency fund while you are working, perhaps you want to consider a 12+ month emergency fund in retirement.

Crunching the retirement savings numbers

To determine how much you need to save each month to fund your retirement, you only need to know the following variables.

- Your current age
- The age you want to retire

- Your Current Income
- Your desired Income replacement ratio
- Your current retirement savings
- Whether or not you have a workplace pension or retirement plan
- How much you are entitled to in government pensions and benefits

The massive impact of workplace pensions and retirement plans

If your employer offers a pension or a matching contribution retirement plan, you need to make sure you are participating and maximizing your benefits, as these tools have a massive impact on your retirement savings plan.

To illustrate the impact workplace retirement plans have on how much you need to save for retirement, let's consider an example under three different scenarios.

1. Where you have no workplace pension or retirement plan.

2. Where you have an employer matching retirement plan.

3. Where you have a defined benefit pension plan.

The assumptions

Let's say you are 35 years old, making $85,000 per year, and want to replace 70% of your income when you retire at 60. Let's also assume you have $60,000 in retirement savings right now. I'll assume your retirement portfolio earns an annual return of 5%.

Finally, these are oversimplified examples that ignore government retirement benefits or other sources of income you might have in retirement.

How much do you need to save for retirement every month?

Scenario 1: No pension or workplace retirement plan

In this scenario, you are entirely on your own when it comes to retirement savings, and to fund your retirement by age 60, you would need to save $2,147 per month to reach your retirement goals.

Scenario 2: Employer Matching retirement plan

If you are lucky enough to have a defined contribution retirement plan or a 401k, the retirement saving math gets much easier.

Let's say your employer matches up to 5% of your salary into a retirement saving plan. Both you and your employer contribute $4,250 per year for a total of $8,500 in annual retirement savings.

You would still need to save $2,147 per month, but your employer would be paying $354 per month through the matching contribution. That means You would need to save $1,793 per month out of your pocket.

Scenario 3: Defined Benefit pension plan

Defined benefit pensions are the ultimate retirement planning tool because a pension is designed to replace a certain percentage of your pre-retirement income. If you have been following along, the entire point of saving for retirement is to replace pre-retirement income, so it's pretty great to have a tool designed to accomplish that exact goal.

The problem with defined benefit pension plans (apart from how few people have them) is that they are very complex. There are a lot of weird formulas and assumptions that go into calculating your pension.

The critical question you will want to ask Human Resources or your company pension committee is what percentage of your income will your pension replace if you retire at your desired retirement age?

If you had a defined benefit pension that will replace 40% of your income when you retire at age 60, then your additional savings would only need to replace 30% of your income (70%-40%).

In this scenario, you would only need to save an additional $720 per month to top up your pension income in retirement.

Government pensions and old-age benefits

Whether or not your workplace offers a pension, it's important to calculate how much you are entitled to from government-sponsored pensions and old-age benefits when you retire.

The more income you expect from government benefits in retirement, the smaller your income replacement ratio needs to be. Every dollar you receive in government retirement benefits is a dollar you will not have to save and replace using your personal retirement savings.

For those in the U.S: The United States Social Security Administration has provided a calculator to help you determine how much you might receive from social security in retirement[22].

For those in Canada: The government of Canada has information reviewing how much income you might expect to receive from the Canadian Pension Plan (CPP) in retirement[23]. The Canadian government has also provided information detailing how much income you might

---

[22] *Quick Calculator*. (2014, May 27). Social Security Quick Calculator. https://www.ssa.gov/OACT/quickcalc/

[23] Service Canada. (2021, September 21). *CPP retirement pension: How much you could receive*. CPP Retirement Pension: How Much You Could Receive. https://www.canada.ca/en/services/benefits/publicpensions/cpp/cpp-benefit/amount.html

expect to receive from Old Age Security (OAS) in retirement[24].

What you need to know to crunch your own retirement savings numbers

Let me teach you exactly how I calculated the monthly retirement savings numbers under each of the above three scenarios. Once you have decided what income level you want to replace in retirement, you only need to calculate two numbers.

1. The lump sum you need to have saved on the day you retire

2. How much do you need to save each month to save up that lump sum

I will teach you how to easily calculate each of these so you can calculate for yourself how much you need to be saving for retirement each month.

The 25 times rule and the 4% rule

The 25 times rule and the 4% rule are two rule of thumb estimates popular in DIY retirement planning.

---

[24] Canada, E. A. S. D. (2021, September 24). *Old Age Security: How much you could receive - Canada.ca*. Old Age Security: How Much You Could Receive. https://www.canada.ca/en/services/benefits/publicpensions/cpp/old-age-security/benefit-amount.html

- The 25 times rule states that you have enough money to retire once you save 25 times your annual living expenses.

- The 4% rule is then used to determine how much of your retirement nest egg you could live off each year.

If your annual expenses were $50,000, the 25 times rule would say you need at least $1,250,000 to retire ($50,000 X 25). If you followed the 4% rule, you could withdraw a maximum of $50,000 per year ($1,250,000 X 4%) and cover your living expenses.

Modifying the 25 times rule to calculate your lump-sum retirement savings

The trouble with the 25 times rule is that it is based on your current living expenses, which, as we have covered, will change dramatically in retirement. You can, however, use the 25 times rule to answer one remaining retirement planning question; "how much money do I need to have saved by the time I retire?"

Returning to our previous example, assuming you have a pre-retirement income of $85,000. You would like to replace 70% or $59,500 of that income in retirement.

Here is how we can use the 25 times rule and 4% rule together to figure out how much money you need to save to provide you $59,500 in income in retirement.

- Multiply your desired retirement income by 25 to arrive at the minimum amount you need to save by retirement. In this example, you need to save $1,487,500 ($59,500 X 25) by the age you wish to retire.

- Then you would use the 4% rule to withdraw $59,500 ($1,487,500 X 0.04) each year in retirement.

Here is a handy DIY retirement formula to determine the minimum amount you need to save to fund your retirement.

Retirement savings goal= (Pre-retirement income X replacement ratio) X 25

This assumes that you are funding your entire retirement from your personal savings, which is not the case for most people. The formula can easily be adapted to reflect how much of your pre-retirement income is covered by pensions and other sources of retirement income.

Returning to our three scenarios above, let's calculate the lump sum required with and without a defined benefit pension. We assume that by the time you retire, your pension will replace 40% of your pre-retirement income, and that means you only need to save a lump sum big enough to cover 30% of your pre-retirement income.

- Lump-sum retirement savings goal (no pension)= ($85,000 X 70%) X 25= $1,487,500

- Lump-sum retirement savings goal (with pension)= ($85,000 X 30%) X 25= $637,500

If you have a pension, subtract the percentage of your income that your pension will replace retirement from your replacement ratio.

Using Excel to calculate your monthly retirement savings

Once you have come up with a lump sum savings goal, you are ready to calculate how much money you need to start saving today to ensure you have that lump sum on the day you retire.

Here is how you can easily calculate how much you need to be saving for retirement each month using Microsoft Excel.

Open up Excel, scroll over to "Functions," and under "Financial," select "PMT."

Click on "PMT," and Excel will open up a panel that looks like this.

Here is how to fill out the field to use the PMT formula to calculate monthly retirement savings.

- **Rate**: Enter the assumed return on retirement invest-ments and divide by 12. In our example, we assumed a 5% rate of return, so under rate, enter "5%/12"

- **Nper**: Enter the number of months until you retire. In our example, we wanted to retire in 25 years, equal to 300 months, so under Nper, enter "300".

- **PV**: Enter the total amount you have saved for retirement right now. In our example, we assumed we had $60,000, so enter "60000" under PV. **Do not enter a comma or use a dollar sign.**

- **FV**: This is the amount of the lump sum we need to save by the time we retire. If you did not have a pension, this was equal to $1,487,500; we will go with that and enter "-1487500". Again enter this number without a comma or dollar sign. **Also, make sure you put a "negative" before the FV number**, or you'll get the wrong result. I know it seems odd, but we are modifying another formula to fit our purposes, so make sure you correctly input everything.

- **Type**: leave this blank.

Hit enter and poof; Excel spits out how much you need to save each month to accumulate a lump sum of $1,487,500 in the next 25 years.

- Without a pension, you need to save $2,147 per month to have a lump-sum savings of $1,487,500 by retirement.

- With a pension, you need to save $2,147 per month to have a lump-sum savings of $637,500 by retirement.

Assumptions, limitations, and a word of caution

The 25 times rule and the 4% rule are "rules of thumb," which means they are never 100% accurate. It's essential to understand the assumptions made in these rules of thumb to understand their limitations better and consider them when determining your DIY retirement plan.

Origins of the 4% rule

The origins of the 4% rule can be traced back to a 1994 paper in the Journal of Financial Planning by William Bengen[25]. In his study, Bengen used U.S data and built a hypothetical portfolio of 50% stocks-50% bonds to find the highest sustainable withdrawal rate for a 30-year retirement.

To do this, he modelled the returns of this portfolio for every 30-year period from 1926 to 1992. He found that a 4% withdrawal rate was the maximum safe withdrawal rate for a 30-year retirement.

In 1998, a second study known as "the trinity study" (named after Trinity University, where the study was done) found similar results as Bengen[26]. The Trinity study

---

[25] Bengen, W. (1994). Determining Safe Withdrawal Rates Using Historical Data. *Journal of Financial Planning*. Published.

[26] Cooley, P. L., Hubbard, C. M., & Walz, D. T. (1998). Retirement Savings: Choosing a Withdrawal Rate That Is Sustainable. *AII Journal*. Published.

found that a 4% withdrawal allowed retirees a 95% chance of not running out of money.

Problems with the 4% rule

The first limitation you need to know about the 25 times and 4% rule is that the research that informs these rules was intended for a 30-year retirement. If you are planning for a retirement longer than 30 years, you run the risk of outliving your money.

The research that informs the 4% rule is focused exclusively on U.S stocks and bonds. Other researchers have had difficulty replicating the 4% rule using international investment data.

Since interest rates are at historic lows, a portfolio would need to be weighed much heavier towards stocks for the 4% rule to hold up. A higher portion of stocks means higher risk and volatility.

An inflexible plan is a bad plan

The fundamental flaw with the 4% rule can be explained in two sentences:

The 4% rule assumes "Average" market returns each year, but there is no such thing as an "average" year in the stock market. A few unlucky years early in your retirement can derail your entire plan.

The last point is critical because the more dependent you are on the stock market to fund your retirement; you expose yourself to the possibility of the market crashing in the first few years of retirement.

Let's say you retire with $1 million invested primarily in the stock market and you plan on using the 4% rule and sell $40,000 worth of assets in year one of retirement.

Then, out of nowhere, the stock market crashes, and your portfolio loses 40% of its value a few months into your retirement. Add in the $40,000 you withdrew to fund your retirement, and after one year, your $1 million retirement nest egg is down to $560,000.

In year two, you increase that $40,000 withdrawal by the rate of inflation, and you keep increasing that withdrawal by the rate of inflation in each subsequent year.

By the time the market finally recovers, you may not have enough money left in your portfolio to ever recover, and your retirement could be in jeopardy.

To quote the great economist, John Maynard Keynes: *"The Market Can Remain Irrational Longer Than You Can Remain Solvent"*

If the market melts down, be prepared to change course

The only reliable retirement plan is one that responds to what's happening in real life.

If the market tanks by 40% in your first year of retirement, you must immediately throw the 4% rule in the garbage. Put simply; you need to have a variable spending plan and adjust your spending in retirement based on what's happening in retirement.

Financial advisor Michael Kitces is the ultimate authority on implementing a variable spending plan. I'll add a footnote to his tremendous blog post explaining this concept in great detail[27].

A variable spending plan is as simple as it sounds.

- If the market goes in the tank, you reduce the amount you withdraw from your portfolio.

- If the market does well, you can choose to increase the amount you withdraw from your portfolio.

If that sounds painfully simple, trust your gut. But you would be shocked at how many people put the blinders on and follow a rigid withdrawal rate regardless of what's happening to their portfolio.

You might be saying: "What if I can't afford to lower my withdrawals without compromising my lifestyle?"

Glad you asked. The answer is more flexibility.

Variable income in retirement

If you can't or won't cut your spending in retirement in response to market volatility, you may also consider a variable income plan in retirement.

---

[27] https://www.kitces.com/blog/the-problem-with-fireing-at-4-and-the-need-for-flexible-spending-rules/

This could be as simple as picking up a part-time job. You'd be amazed at how much easier life would be in retirement with even a little bit of income that's independent of your portfolio.

That's exactly why you would want to consider building a second-income stream through a side hustle. If you can pay for your living expenses doing work you love, then you may never choose to retire.

But it's still critical to have at least a base retirement plan in place because here are two more things we can't predict:

- What your health will be like in the future.
- What the economy will be like in the future.

Even if you love what you do, there is no guarantee you'll be able to continue doing it forever. But there is one undeniable truth about retirement planning: The longer you work, the less likely you are to outlive your money.

Chapter Recap

Remember the 4-steps to figuring out how much you need to save for retirement.

1. Decide how much income you will need in retirement.

2. Determine how much money you need to have saved on the day you retire to generate your retirement income.

3. Calculate how much you need to start saving right now.

4. Ensure your success by automating your savings.

- The amount of income you'll need to replace in retirement will be determined by which living expenses will go up and which will go down in retirement, and by how much. A 70% replacement ratio is commonly used and is a fine starting point in your analysis.

- How much money you need to have saved by the time you retire is determined by the withdrawal rate you choose. A 4% withdrawal rate is commonly used, but it's important to customize a withdrawal rate that fits your circumstances.

- Once you know how much you need to save each month to fund your retirement, lock in your success by automating your savings.

Chapter 9:

The Biggest Financial Risk You'll Face in Life

When I ask people what they believe to be the largest asset they own, most people think it's their house or retirement portfolio. Those people would be wrong.

Unless you are nearing retirement, your largest asset is your human capital, AKA your ability to make money.

Human capital makes all other investments possible. It is the engine of our financial lives. If we agree that there is no financial issue more important than our human capital, then losing it is the biggest financial risk we all face.

In this chapter, I will put my "economist hat" on and nerd out about personal finance and how to think about managing risk in your life.

But don't go anywhere! I know that might sound boring, but if you are at all interested in personal finance, then I think you will really enjoy this discussion. I assure you that you will take away a few *useful nuggets that will make it worth your time.*

Putting a dollar figure on your human capital

If you're not sold on the idea that your human capital is your greatest asset, allow me to prove it to you quickly.

In finance, there is a term called "Present Value", which tells us how much a lump sum or a series of cashflow received in the future is worth today.

Since your human capital is simply all the paychecks you expect to receive during your working life, it is a series of future cashflows, and we can apply a Present Value to it.

The Present Value to your human capital is how much money I would need to give you today to never work another day in your life and have you been just as well off financially.

The younger you are, the larger the Present Value of your human capital is. This is because you have more future paychecks to collect than someone nearing retirement.

If you're under the age of 30, there is a very high probability that the present value of your human capital is worth millions.

You're sitting on a gold mine

A gold mine is the best analogy I have heard for describing your human capital.

You are sitting on a substantial amount of wealth. The only problem is that, like with a gold mine, you can't extract that wealth all at once. You need to go in and mine the gold bit by bit. For most of us, we only get a small piece of gold every two weeks on payday.

Then, as you age, the gold begins to slowly deplete; there is only a finite amount of gold to mine. One day, the gold will run out. In the case of your human capital, you retire and have no more paychecks left to collect.

Our biggest financial risk is losing our human capital

If you agree with me that your ability to earn an income is your greatest asset, then losing it is your greatest financial risk.

When most people think of "losing their ability to earn income", they think of losing their job, getting fired, or being laid off.

A job loss can be devastating, but it does not represent a permanent loss of your human capital. Returning to the gold mine analogy, think of losing a job as a temporary halt in mining operations.

The only way to permanently lose your human capital is for you to die prematurely.

Yes, we are going to talk about life insurance. It's A topic we hate to discuss, but it's incredibly important for anyone who has people that depend on them financially, so we are going to talk about it, and I'll do my best to make it fun.

The gold mine that is your human capital is not only a benefit to you but to your family and anyone else who depends on you for financial support.

If you die prematurely, your family loses access to that gold deposit forever. Depending on your age and your income, that could mean they lose out on millions in future income.

I'm 32 years old, a new father, and I make above-average income; I am sitting on a gold mine of human capital worth millions. But it means nothing to my son if I were to die tomorrow because the value of my human capital would instantly drop to $0.

There is no greater financial risk for me, so as uncomfortable as it is to confront, I have no choice.

The perfect hedge against losing your human capital

Luckily, there is a simple way to hedge against the permanent loss of your human capital, and the best news is that it is generally very cheap.

Term life insurance is the perfect way to manage the risk of dying prematurely.

Term life insurance and your human capital have a perfect negative correlation; if one pays out this year, the other will not.

- If you die this year, your life insurance policy will pay out, but you won't collect any human capital.

- If you don't die, you'll continue collecting human capital, but the life insurance policy won't pay out a dime to your family.

Why term life insurance and not permanent life insurance?

There are two types of life insurance:

1. Term life insurance.

2. Permanent life insurance.

Term life insurance is very cheap but only grants you coverage for a specified period of time, such as 10 or 20 years.

Permanent life insurance is more expensive but lasts your whole life. As long as you continue making the premium payments, you'll have coverage.

I am very specific in saying that term life insurance is the perfect hedge to your human capital.

Term life insurance is very cheap when you are young, which allows you to buy more of it. As you age and you need to renew your term life insurance policy, it will get more expensive.

This perfectly matches the progression of your human capital.

- When you are young, the Present Value of your human capital is large, so you need more insurance.
- As you age, the present value of your human capital decreases, so you need less insurance.

There are only two reasons someone would need to have permanent life insurance:

1. They want to ensure they leave a financial inheritance.
2. They are in a high tax bracket and want to do some advanced financial planning strategies.

For the purpose of our discussion on managing the risk of losing your human capital, cheap term life insurance is the perfect solution.

The happy news is that during the period of your life where you need it the most, term life insurance is very cheap. It has become a highly commoditized product with lots of new businesses entering the industry, which has pushed costs down.

According to a report from ValuePenguin[28], the average cost for a 20-year term life insurance policy with a $500,000 death benefit is $126 per month.

A lot of you might read that and say, "I can't afford $126 per month!"

I know $126 is not an insignificant amount of money. If you don't have any financial dependents and you're on a tight budget, it makes sense that life insurance is not an immediate priority.

However, if you have a family who depends on the income you provide through your human capital, and you're asking if you can afford term life insurance, my question to you is: **how can you afford not to have it**?

Chapter Recap

- Your human capital is the most important asset you will ever own.

- Unless you are independently wealthy, you need life insurance if you have people that are financially dependent on your income.

- Term life insurance is the perfect hedge against dying prematurely and your family losing your future human capital forever.

---

[28] Price, S. (2021, March 5). *Average Cost of Life Insurance (2021): Rates by Age, Term and Policy Size*. ValuePenguin. https://www.valuepenguin.com/average-cost-life-insurance#:%7E:text=We%27ve%20found%20that%20the,a%20death%20benefit%20of%20%24500%2C000.

Chapter 10:

The Goals Based Budget

Your whole life, people have been telling you how important it is to have a budget. If budgets are so important, then why do 60% of people not have one[29]?

The reason so few people use a budget is that most budgets are arbitrary templates that are not based on people's individual goals or circumstances. It feels too much like a chore, so people simply don't stick to their budget.

A budget is an opportunity to write down your financial priorities

A budget is simply a reflection of your financial priorities. If you chose to budget for saving for retirement, you are declaring that it is a financial priority. Conversely, by not including something in your budget, you are declaring that item is not a priority.

Creating a budget is a worthwhile exercise because it forces you to prioritize your financial goals. By the time

---

[29] Fool, M. B. F. T. M. (2016, October 24). *Nearly 3 in 5 Americans are making this huge financial mistake*. CNNMoney. https://money.cnn.com/2016/10/24/pf/financial-mistake-budget/index.html

you get through paying for your big 3 living expenses, odds are you won't have a lot of money left over for other goals.

If you love to travel and want to save to buy a house but only have $500 left over at the end of the month, how do you allocate that money; to the house or to travel? The answer will reveal which option is a bigger priority for you.

Why many people can't stick to a budget

The reason most people quit on their budget is that they are following a budget template. When you follow a budget template, you aren't budgeting for your financial priorities, you are budgeting based on someone else's financial priorities.

For example, the 50/20/30 rule is one of the most popular budget templates.

Here's how a 50/20/30 budget works.

- 50% of your money should be spent on "needs".
- 30% of your money should be spent on "wants".
- 20% of your money should go to saving and investing.

Don't get me wrong; budget templates like the **50/20/30 rule** are useful if your spending is out of control, and you quickly need to make some necessary changes to your finances. But once you have your spending under control, a template budget can begin to feel like a chore. Once it starts to feel like a chore, that's when most people drop their budget.

What I do instead of following a strict budget

I've always liked the concept of "paying yourself first". This simply means that before you pay any bills or spend any money, you set aside a portion of your paycheck and save it.

Saving could mean a lot of things, it could mean saving in an emergency fund, for retirement, paying down debt or saving for a specific goal like buying a house or your child's education.

I take the pay yourself first approach to budgeting. Rather than adhering to arbitrary spending rules like spending 20% of my income on wants, **I figure out how much money I need to save each month to accomplish my financial goals, automate that savings process, and spend whatever is left over.**

I refer to this loose form of budgeting as a **goals-based** budget.

How to set up a goals-based budget in 6 steps:

1. **List out your financial priorities**. For example, saving for retirement.

2. **Set goals around each priority**. For example, I would like to be able to retire by 65.

3. **Figure out how much you need to save each month to accomplish those goals**. For example, to retire at 65, I might need to save $800 per month toward retirement.

4. **Figure out if you have enough money to accomplish each goal**. For example, maybe after paying for your necessary living expenses like rent and groceries, you discover you only have $500 left over to save toward retirement.

5. **Make adjustments to free up more money or review and set less aggressive goals**. If you were $300 short of your monthly retirement savings goal, you might look for $300 worth of spending you can cut, find a way to make $300 more each month, or push back your retirement age based on being able to save $500 rather than $800.

6. **Automate your savings**. Once you land on savings goals, you can afford, ensure you achieve those goals by automating your savings.

An example of a goals-based budget

Step 1: List your financial priorities

In this example of building a goals-based budget, I will assume you have three top financial priorities.

1. Build an emergency fund.
2. Pay off debt.
3. Save for retirement.

Step 2: Set goals based on your priorities

Once you have established your financial priorities, it's essential to set some SMART goals around those priorities. By SMART, I mean:

- Specific
- Measurable
- Attainable
- Realistic
- Timely

Merely saying, "I want to get out of debt," is not a SMART goal. Saying, "I want to get out of debt in three years using the avalanche method to debt repayment," is an example of a SMART goal.

Based on the three financial priorities above, here is an example of 3 goals:

1. Having a 6-month emergency fund saved up in the next 12-months.
2. Having all non-mortgage debt paid off in the next three years, using the avalanche method.
3. Saving enough every month to have the option of retiring by the age of 65.

Step 3: Figure out how much you need to save each month to accomplish those goals

Having a goal is nice, knowing how much you need to save to accomplish those goals is the next step to making them become a reality.

Building a 6-month emergency fund in the next 12-months

Figuring out how much you need to save in your emergency fund is a three-step process.

- Step 1: Track your spending and figure out how much you spend on essential expenses each month.

- Step 2: Decide how many months you would like your emergency fund to cover your essential expenses.

- Step 3: Multiply the amount in step 1 by the number in step 2. This tells you the total size emergency fund you need in place. Subtract how much you already have saved for an emergency fund.

- Step 4: Set a goal for how many months you would like to have your emergency fund fully funded.

- Divide the total in step 3 by the number of months in step 4.

Here's a quick example to illustrate how this works:

- Step 1: After tracking your expenses, you learn you spend $2,040 per month on essential expenses like housing, transportation, food, and utilities. You also spend $460 on the minimum payments on all your debts. That brings you up to $2,500 per month on essential expenses.

- Step 2: You decide you want your emergency fund to cover 6 months' worth of essential expenses.

- Step 3: That means you need $15,000 saved in an emergency fund. Let's say you currently have $3,000 saved in an emergency fund. That means you still need to save $12,000.

- Step 4: Recall your goal to have a fully funded emergency fund in 12-months.

- Step 5: **That means you need to save $1,000 per month over the next 12-months to achieve your goal.**

Having all non-mortgage debt paid off in the next three years, using the avalanche method

Let's assume you have the following non-mortgage debts:

- A credit card with a $3,000 balance, a 20% interest rate, and a $60 minimum monthly payment.

- A car loan with a $10,000 balance, a 6% interest rate, and a $300 minimum monthly payment.

- A personal loan with a $5,000 balance, an 8.5% interest rate, and a $100 minimum monthly payment.

Using the avalanche method, you pay off your debts in order of the loan with the highest rate of interest to the lowest rate of interest. That means the order in which you would pay off your debt would be as follows:

- Credit card
- Personal loan
- Car loan

To pay each of these debts off in three years using the avalanche method would mean you would need to pay $585 toward your debt each month.

- First, you would pay $185 toward the credit card while maintaining the minimum payments on the car and personal loans. In 20-months, you would have the credit card paid off.

- Next, you would pay $273.45 toward the personal loan and maintain the minimum payment on the car loan. By month 33, the personal loan would be paid off.

- Finally, you would pay $585 toward the car loan. By month 36 (three years), the car loan would be paid off.

Saving enough every month to have the option of retiring by the age of 65

When putting together a DIY retirement savings plan, there are several vital variables you need to consider:

- Years until retirement.

- How long you expect to live.

- Percentage of pre-retirement income you would like to have in retirement.

- Workplace retirement plans and pensions.

- Government benefits and pensions.

- Assumed return on investment for your retirement portfolio.

- How much money you currently have saved for retirement.

Let's assume the following in our example:

- You're 35 years old.

- You would like to retire at 65.

- You currently make $70,000 per year and would like to have 70% of that income in retirement.

- Current retirement savings total $100,000.

- At work, you have access to a defined contribution retirement plan where you and your employer each contribute 8% of your salary into a retirement plan.

- You assume a 5% rate of return on your retirement portfolio.

Based on all the assumptions made above, in this example, you would need to save an additional $322 in addition to what you and your employer contribute to your retirement savings plan.

Totalling up the amount needed to save for all three financial goals:

- Monthly savings into emergency fund: $1,000 (for 12 months)

- Monthly payments on debt: $585 (for 3 years)
- Monthly retirement savings: $322 (for 30 years)

Total amount needed each month to accomplish your three financial goals: $1,907

Step 4: Figure out if you have enough money to accomplish all your goals

The crucial question after figuring out how much money you would need to set aside to accomplish your goals is if you can afford it.

- Step 1: Calculate your monthly take-home pay.
- Step 2: Subtract the amount needed to accomplish your goals.
- Step 3: Subtract the amount of money needed to pay for your essential living expenses.
- Step 4: Track your expenses and determine the minimum amount you could spend on variable expenses (good thing we already covered this at the beginning of the book). Subtract this from your take-home pay as well.
- Step 5: If you are left with a positive number, you are in good shape. If you are left with a negative number, there is more work to be done.

Returning to our example, here is how that process would work:

- Step 1: Let's assume on a $70,000 annual salary, you clear $4,333 per month after taxes and deductions.

- Step 2: After accounting for the $1,907 you need to accomplish your financial goals, you are left with $2,426.

- Step 3: After subtracting $2,040 needed for your essential living expenses, you are left with $386.

- Step 4: After tracking your spending, you determine that the lowest level of non-essential expenses you would be comfortable with is $1,000.

- Step 5: That would leave you with a $614 monthly budget deficit.

Clearly, there is more work to be done.

Step 5: Make adjustments as needed

If, after creating your goals based budget, you find you can't afford to pay for your living expenses and save toward your financial goals, you have four options to balance your budget:

1. **Increase your take-home pay**. Perhaps by taking on a side hustle or working overtime hours.

2. **Live more frugally**. The low hanging fruit to cut spending would be to look at your big-3 spending of housing, transportation, and food.

3. **Rework your goals to make them less aggressive**. For example, if you push your retirement age from 65 to 68, you could free up over $200 per month.

4.   **Prioritize your goals**. If you still can't make the budget work, it might be time to prioritize your goals. For example, you might want to focus on building your emergency fund before getting aggressive on debt or saving for retirement. The good news is that, once your emergency fund is fully funded, you no longer need to save for it every month. In this example, that would free up $1,000 per month.

Through some combination of the above four options, you can balance your goals-based budget.

Step 6: Automate your savings

Saying that you are going to prioritize and save for your goals is an excellent first step. However, there is still a big liability you'll have to deal with: yourself. Everyone has noble intentions when it comes to budgeting and saving. Still, many people lack the discipline to maintain their savings plans over the long term.

That is why I am a big fan of automating as much of my financial life as possible. By doing so, I take the savings decision out of my hand.

Most banks allow you to easily set up an automated withdrawal from your checking account on every payday and have that money placed in a savings or investment account. This will ensure that you follow through on your savings plan because there are no further decisions required on your part.

The other great thing about automating your savings and debt repayment is that, eventually you won't even notice the money is gone. The money is never in your checking account long enough for you to spend. After a while, you adjust your spending as if that money was never there.

Chapter Recap

- Budgeting is important because it forces you to prioritize your financial goals.

- A budget template can be a good way to get started, especially if you need help reigning in your spending.

- However, many people find it challenging to stick with budget templates for the long term. The simple reason is that your life is not a template. If you're going to stick with a budget for the long term, it should allow for more flexible spending.

- That is why I am a fan of the goals-based budgeting approach, which is a six-step process.

- Step 1: List out your financial priorities.

- Step 2: Set goals around each priority.

- Step 3: Figure out how much you need to save each month to accomplish those goals.

- Step 4: Figure out if you have enough money to accomplish each goal.

- Step 5: Make adjustments to free up more money or review and set less aggressive goals.

- Step 6 Automate your savings and spend whatever is left over; however you please.

The final thought I'll leave you with is to remind you that the goals-based budget process should be reviewed and adjusted periodically. As your goals change, so must your budget.

Once you start achieving financial goals, you will have an important decision to make: what to do with the money you were saving toward the goal that has now been accomplished. Ideally, you will reallocate that money toward new goals that will help you live a prosperous and happy life.

Part 2:

The Financial Freedom Equation

Chapter 11:

A Simple Definition of Financial Freedom

I have a very simple definition of financial freedom:

You have achieved financial freedom when you can spend your days doing work that you love without worrying about how you will pay the bills.

I think of this as my mission statement for managing my money and my career. I don't want to retire. I want to keep working, possibly forever. I just want to be in a position where I can choose:

- What projects I work on.

- When I start and stop working.

- Who I choose to work with.

- Where I do that work.

Most importantly, I want all of that without worrying about financial stress from having a bad month or two.

If that sounds like a high bar, that's because it is. **High bars lead to a better life**. The most miserable time in my life was when I set the bar so low that paying my rent and having money to go to the movies was considered a *good month*.

Financial freedom is a high bar, but we should all strive for it because it is one that we all have the capacity to clear. In this chapter, I will discuss how to get started.

The financial freedom equation

If you want to do the work you love without ever having to worry about money, you simply need to solve the financial freedom equation:

Financial Freedom = (Income from work you love + Passive income) > Your living expenses

That's it.

If you can make enough money through a combination of passive income and money doing work you love to cover your living expenses, financial freedom can be yours.

Over the next few chapters, I'll break each piece of that equation down further.

Chapter 12:

You Need Exactly 2 Income Streams

One of the popular topics in personal finance is having multiple streams of income.

The argument goes like this:

Our human capital aka our ability to earn an income is our most important asset in life. Therefore, diversifying your human capital by having multiple streams of income is a smart way to manage risk.

Great! Multiple streams of income; got it! But how many income streams is best? There are many different ways of thinking about this. I've read articles arguing for five or more income streams.

In this chapter, I make the case for why you need exactly two income streams. No more, no less.

The best emergency fund is one you never need to use

Let's start with a shared definition of the term "*income stream*". I define an income stream as follows:

A unique source of monthly income to reliably cover your living expenses.

So, if you need $4,000 per month to fund your lifestyle, we will not count a side hustle that makes $600 per month. If you want to build an unbreakable financial position, you want two unique sources of income that can reliably cover your living expenses. That $600 per month side hustle will make life easier for you and could one day grow into a full income stream, but until it does, we can't rely on it.

As we discussed in part 1 of this book, one of the most classic pieces of financial advice is to have 3–6 months' worth of living expenses set aside in cash in case you were to lose your job. This is a strong financial defensive move.

In sports, some say the best defense is a strong offense, which can also apply to our finances. If you have a side hustle that can cover your living expenses, you could lose your day job and never end up needing to tap into your emergency fund. I am not saying you don't need a strong emergency fund, but the best emergency fund is one you never need to touch. Having two streams of income that can fully cover your living expenses is the easiest way to accomplish that.

My two streams of income are helping me build a third

Right now, I have two unique sources of income that can cover my living expenses:

1. My day job.

2. My side hustle.

The real beauty of having these two income streams is that they are helping me build a third stream of income—passive income from investments.

Generating enough passive income to cover your living expenses is hard and takes most people their entire lives. The only way to shorten the amount of time it takes to build that much passive income is by maximizing your savings rate, which is the percentage of your take-home pay that you save and invest every month.

That's where having two streams of income is powerful because, by definition, it means you'll be able to achieve a minimum savings rate of 50% if you dedicate one of your income streams to saving and investing. If one or more of your income streams is enough to more than cover your living expenses, you can accelerate your savings rate.

By keeping my living expenses constant and constantly looking for ways to increase my current income streams, I've been able to invest a decent amount of money *relative to my living expenses*.

That last point is the key to generating enough passive income to cover your living expenses.

It's not how much money you have invested that counts, it's how much you have invested relative to your living expenses.

- $1 million could last a lifetime if you only need $30,000 per year.

- $1 million can evaporate pretty quickly if you
  need $300,000 per year.

So, right now, I am taking all my surplus money from
my day job and side hustle and investing it. Once I have
reached the point where my passive investment income
can reliably cover my living expenses, I plan on dropping one of my current income streams.

Why not three or more streams of income?

Once my side hustle/writing career grew into a second-
ary income stream, I got way too excited and tried setting up endless streams of new income:

- Online courses.

- Subscription newsletters.

- YouTube videos.

- A podcast.

Other than the online courses, none of these other income
streams amounted to much.

**The real problem was that I was spreading myself too
thin. This began to impact my enjoyment of my day
job and the profitability of my writing side hustle.**

I learned the hard way that my human capital has dimin-
ishing returns at a certain point. Since my side hustle of
writing provided scalable income, I was best served to focus

on writing rather than these other income streams that all demand time and energy, which are finite resources.

One day, when one of my income streams is passive income from my investments, it might make sense for me to pursue some of these other income streams.

It doesn't cost me any time or energy to receive a dividend from my stock portfolio, so this provides an exception to my rule of two income streams. If one of your income streams is passive investment income, you might choose to maintain three income streams or drop your day job or side hustle and spend more time enjoying life.

Chapter 13:

4 Things Every Successful Side Hustler Needs Clarity On

The first time you make a dollar from something you've created is one of the most powerful feelings in the world. It's also a dangerous moment.

It really can be a mind-expanding experience. You begin to imagine what life would be like to spend all your work time creating things you care about. The first time I started to believe that could be my future, it lit a fire under my ass. I was ready to do whatever I needed to do to make that dream a reality.

The problem was that I had no idea exactly what it was I "*needed to do*". I opted for the "buckshot approach" to content creation.

- Since I found success writing personal finance articles, why not repurpose those ideas and bring them to YouTube or podcasting?

- Why not write about other topics I'm interested in, like movies and sports?

My problem was that I had no clarity on who I was as a creator, so I ended up spinning around in frustrating circles.

Today, I have clarity on who I am as a creator and what I need to do to scale my income as a creator, to make this my full-time reality and not just a side hustle.

Here are four things any creator needs clarity on if they ever hope to earn a living from their creative genius:

#1 — What type of content creator are you?

My background is in economics, and I use that knowledge as a creator in a topic I care deeply about: personal finance.

When it comes to investing, which is an important aspect of personal finance, one of the most important things you can do is to diversify your portfolio. I don't invest in any individual stocks; I diversify by buying all the stocks through low-cost index funds as we discussed earlier in the book. I do this because there is a mountain of evidence that suggests this is the most rational way to invest my money.

The first time I made $1,000 in a month from writing about personal finance, I had a very terrible idea— I thought I should diversify my income as a creator in the same way I do my investment portfolio.

I told myself this was a "*rational*" and "*strategic*" decision, but really it was a fear-based decision, which I should know, as a personal finance writer, typically leads to bad outcomes.

I was afraid that if my writing career began to plateau or I lost my audience, I would be finished as a profitable creator. So, I decided to diversify my income streams as a creator by starting a YouTube channel, a podcast, a paid newsletter, and online courses.

I did this all at the same time while also learning how to be a new father and working a 9-to-5 job.

I told myself I was diversifying, but what I was doing was spreading myself too thin and undermining my own success and depriving my audience of the thing that drew them to me in the first place— personal finance articles.

The moment I accepted that I am a writer, not a video creator or a podcaster, was a revelatory moment.

Stop and ask yourself: what type of creator am I?

#2 — What subject area do you have expert knowledge in?

Even after I accepted that "*I am a writer*", I couldn't get this terrible idea of diversification out of my head. I couldn't shake certain thoughts like, "*what if I run out of financial topics to write about?*"

So, I made another stupid decision which was to diversify the topics I write about. I like movies and sports, so I started writing a few articles about those subjects.

You might be thinking that I am stubborn as hell. I (and my wife) would agree with you.

Luckily, I snapped out of the delusion that I could start from scratch and become an expert writer on three different topics at the same time.

The next great clarity as a creator came when I accepted another fact: I am a personal finance writer.

That doesn't mean I won't write about other topics on occasion because I do. **But I never lose sight of what drives my economic engine as a creator – writing about personal finance.**

What is the one subject that can drive your economic engine as a creator?

#3 — Who do you create for?

When I first got started as a writer, I wrote for an audience of one– *myself.*

In some ways, I still do that. When I notice recurring thoughts or ideas are swirling in my head, I write about them. This process has yielded some of the most popular articles I've ever written.

- When I started noticing articles and videos all over the internet pushing false claims of "*passive income*", I wrote about why passive income shouldn't be your focus.

- When I grew tired of the endless debates in the personal finance community about homeownership, I wrote my definitive take on the issue in a 4,000-word article that encompassed all my thoughts on the good, the bad, and the ugly of home ownership.

So, yes, I write about the issues that preoccupy my thoughts, but when I sit down to write the article, I try to write it for one of two target audiences:

1. People who are new to personal finance and can be easily swayed by clickbait articles and hyped-up "*get rich quick*" ideas.

2. People who have all the basics of personal finance down and are looking to "level up" with money and begin to leverage that wealth into more freedom.

Whenever you create a new piece of content, it's important to ask yourself: *who needs to hear this?*

#4 — What's your scalable product?

Earlier in this book, I wrote about the importance of "*scalable income*" as a creator or side hustler. This simply means having a product to sell that allows you to control your income.

If you can control your income, you control your future.

The obvious question for any creator is, "*What should my product be?*"

It could be an online course, software, a digital product, or a paid newsletter, just to name a few possibilities. How do you know which is the right choice for you?

Once you have clarity on the first three topics we've discussed in this chapter, it won't be hard to find clarity on what your product should be.

Once I had clarity on what type of content creator I am (a writer), what subject area I have expert knowledge in (personal finance), and who I'm writing for, it became instantly clear to me that my scalable product should be a personal finance book (the one you're reading right now).

If you have clarity on who you are as a creator, where your expertise lies, and who you want to help, it won't be difficult to develop the product that will allow you to own your income and make a good living as a creator.

Do this for yourself, because financial freedom is doing work you love without worrying about how you'll pay the bills.

But do it for the rest of us because the world needs more people pouring their energy into things that matter.

Chapter 14:

You Need to Understand What Passive Income Is (And Isn't)

This is a big important topic. Let's start by referring back to the financial freedom equation:

Financial Freedom = (Income from work you love + passive income) > Your living expenses

In this chapter, we are going to tackle the issue of "passive income".

Passive income is one of the most frequently misused terms in personal finance.

There is no shortage of internet marketers that want to sell you on the idea that if you simply listen to them (and buy their "program"), you too can kick back and start generating income with minimal effort.

Here's the thing, the idea of passive income is a load of crap.

That doesn't mean that you can't start a digital business and change your financial life forever because you absolutely can and should. We just talked about why having two income streams is so important to reach financial freedom.

Usually, when you hear someone refer to "*passive income*", what they really mean is a business with scalable income. Scalable income means you are not guaranteed to make a dime, but there is no limit on your earning potential.

An example of how scalable income works

The book you are currently reading is a perfect example of scalable income.

- If no one buys my book, I won't make any money.

- Since it is a digital product, it does not cost me extra money to sell additional books.

- This is in stark contrast to someone selling physical goods.

- If I was selling computers, I would incur extra costs for every computer I sold. In economics, this is referred to as the "*marginal cost of production*".

- Selling a digital product, especially an info-product like a book means my marginal cost of production is next to nothing.

- That means my costs would be the same if I sold zero or 1 million books.

That is what it means to have scalable income, and it is what most people refer to as "*passive income*".

And while it is true that you may need to work less for every additional dollar of scalable income, it's not like you can just kick your feet up and stop working. Passive income is money you can earn without doing any work. If I stopped working on my business, it wouldn't be long before the income dried up.

The only true source of passive income comes from investment income. Which leads us to the first rule about passive income.

Passive income cannot exist without active income

Active income means having a job, a side hustle or a full-time business. You work, get paid, and invest whatever money is left over at the end of the month. Those investments are what will generate passive income.

You may have noticed that I have repeatedly mentioned the importance of investing in this book, but I haven't gone into detail on "how" to invest your money. That is exactly what we are going to discuss in the next chapter.

Chapter 15:

A Beginner's Guide to Passive Investing

With the rise of low-cost index fund ETFs and online brokerages, there has never been a better time to be a DIY index investor. The issue holding many would-be investors back is, they don't know where to get started.

To get started and become a successful DIY index investor, you simply need to know a few basics.

- **The difference between good index funds and "fake" index funds**

- **Whether or not it makes sense for you to use a robo-advisor or go the pure DIY route.**

- **How to figure out your risk tolerance and set up a risk-appropriate portfolio.**

- **How to diversify your investment portfolio.**

- **Which online brokerage to pick.**

- **How to actually buy index funds.**

Let's dive into each of these topics.

What are index funds and ETFs?

Let's start with some basic terminology.

- Index funds are funds that replicate an index of assets like stocks or bonds. For example, an S&P 500 index fund replicates the S&P 500 index, which is a list of the 505 largest companies in the U.S. as measured by their market capitalization.

- ETFs or Exchange Traded Funds are investment funds that can be bought and sold on stock exchanges in the same way as individual stocks.

What is the difference between index funds and ETFs?

Many people think that index funds and ETFs are the same, but they are not.

- Index funds are defined by their passive investment strategy of replicating a particular index of assets.

- ETFs are defined as a specific structure of an investment fund.

Not all Index funds are ETFs, and not all ETFs are index funds.

- Many index funds are not ETFs but structured as traditional mutual funds. This means they are not bought on stock exchanges but directly through investment fund companies.

- Many ETFs do not follow an indexing strategy. This means they have active fund managers picking and choosing assets rather than following a passive investment strategy.

It is essential to understand the critical differences between index funds and ETFs. However, **for the purpose of this discussion, when I refer to "index funds", I am referring to ETF index funds**. Since this is a guide to becoming a *"DIY index investor"* and ETF index funds are much more accessible compared to index mutual funds, this is a guide specifically about investing in ETF index funds.

Index funds do not refer only to stocks

When many people hear the term "index fund", they think of an index fund that tracks the stock market. However, there are index funds that track many different asset classes. The two most popular asset classes for index investors are stocks and bonds, so we will focus on those assets for the remainder of this discussion.

Not all index funds are created equal

One of the most important things for any new investor to know is that just because an ETF is called an "index fund" does not mean it is a good investment.

There are more indexes and index ETFs than I could ever keep track of. Let's simplify things by separating index funds into two categories:

1. Broad-based index funds.

2. Niche index funds.

Broad-based index funds invest in all or most of a particular asset class in a specific geographic region. An S&P 500 index fund, invests in the majority of the U.S. stock market. These are "good" index funds.

Niche based index funds invest in "*alternative*" assets and subsections of a broad-based index. For example, you could invest in an index fund that tracks an index of technology companies. These are risky investments.

Niche index funds, by their nature, are much more concentrated than broad-based index funds and therefore have a higher variance in possible outcomes. They could do great, or they could do terrible.

There are two types of risk investors should be aware of:

1. Systematic risk.

2. Idiosyncratic risk.

Systematic risk is the risk that the entire economy and stock market will experience a downturn. Systematic risk is something anyone investing in the stock market accepts.

They accept this risk because the expected (not guaranteed) outcome of investing in stocks is positive. This is where the term "no risk, no reward" comes from.

Idiosyncratic risk is the risk that faces an individual company (for those who pick stocks) or a specific sector (for those who choose niche index funds) but not the entire market.

For example, if you invested in a technology index fund, you would be exposed to the broader stock market risk and risks that are specific to the technology industry.

Idiosyncratic risks can be managed through proper diversification. By proper diversification, I mean investing in broad-based index funds that are diversified by asset class and geography (more on that later).

If your goal is to maximize risk-adjusted expected returns, broad-based index funds make much more sense than buying niche index funds.

Why invest in index funds at all?

While this chapter is dedicated to understanding "how" to invest in index funds, it's worth discussing "why" someone would invest in index funds.

To put it in the simplest terms, index investing is the simplest, lowest cost, most rational way for the majority of people to invest their money.

Using equity index funds as an example, investing in a total stock market index fund is the simplest way to invest in stocks. You don't need to know a lot about finance or think about what you're invested in. That's why it's called "passive" investing.

If you buy a total stock market index fund, you're invested in every single company in the stock market. If someone were to ask you what stocks you're invested in, your reply would be "all of them". It does not get any simpler than that.

Index funds are the cheapest way to build a diversified investment portfolio.

- Buying individual stocks typically comes with high transaction costs.

- Buying an actively managed investment fund comes with annual investment fees known as Management Expense Ratios (MER), often in the range of 1%-2% of your investments, meaning if you invested $100,000, you would pay $1,000–$2,000 per year in fees.

- Index funds, on the other hand, are incredibly cheap. For example, Vanguard's S&P 500 index fund has an MER of 0.03%, meaning if you invested $100,000, you would pay $30 per year in fees.

Index funds are also the most rational way to invest, particularly if you're investing in stocks. I don't say this based on my opinion; I say this because it is what the majority of academic research suggests to be true.

Eugene Fama, an economics professor from the University of Chicago, is best known for his work on the efficient market theory[30], which states that stock prices are unpredictable and reflect all available information. It should be noted that Fama won the Nobel Prize in Economics for his work on efficient market theory[31].

If stock prices reflect all available information, and we can't predict how their price will change in the future, it's next to impossible for investors to consistently outperform the average return of the stock market.

Even if we accept that markets are not perfectly efficient, they are efficient enough that 75% of active fund managers in the U.S underperformed the S&P 500 index over the past five years[32].

Investing in index funds is simple, cheap, and has outperformed the vast majority of wall street investment fund managers. It sounds like a pretty rational way to invest if you ask me.

---

[30] Fama, E. (1970). Efficient Capital Markets: A Review of Theory and Empirical Work. *The Journal of Finance, 25*(2), 383-417. doi:10.2307/2325486

[31] *Nobel Prizes 2020*. (2013). NobelPrize.Org. https://www.nobelprize.org/prizes/economic-sciences/2013/fama/facts/

[32] *Spiva - S&P Dow Jones Indices*. (2021). S&P Dow Jones Indices. https://www.spglobal.com/spdji/en/research-insights/spiva/#/reports

Your biggest risk as an index investor is yourself

We've talked about systematic risk and idiosyncratic risk. Now it's time to discuss the greatest investment risk of all: **you**.

Index funds are designed to be passive investments, meaning you buy index funds and hold them for an extended period of time. That is the right way to invest.

The wrong way to invest in index funds is to continually buy and sell them based on what you "think" is going to happen in the stock market. Morning start published a report that found investors consistently underperform the funds they were invested in by nearly 1% per year during that time[33].

- The average fund in the study returned 7.05% per year.

- Meanwhile, the average investor returned 6.1% per year.

You might think to yourself, how is it possible for a fund to return 7%, but investors in that fund only realized a 6% return?

---

[33] Kinnel, R. (2016, May 23). *Mind the Gap: Why Investors Lag Funds.* Morningstar, Inc. https://www.morningstar.com/articles/582626/mind-the-gap-why-investors-lag-funds

To understand the answer to that question, think about how many investors behave when things get choppy in the stock market.

- The stock market sees a sharp sell-off, like in the 2008–2009 financial crisis. Investors get scared and sell at the bottom. This turns paper losses into real losses.

- Then, they sit on the sidelines and watch as the stock market recovers. Since the stock market often recovers faster than the economy, investors miss out on some of the best months to be invested in the stock market.

- Once the economy recovers, investors feel "safe" to get back into the stock market, and they buy when prices are high.

In short, many investors sell-low and buy-high, which is the exact recipe to underperform the funds they are invested in.

If you're saving for a long-term goal like retirement, that is many years or decades away, what happens in the day to day of the stock market should be of little concern. More money is lost in trying and failing to time the market than when market declines itself.

Index funds are passive investments, but only if you treat them that way by buying and holding rather than trying to time the market.

How to properly diversify an index portfolio

When building your portfolio, you'll want to consider reducing risk through diversification. There are two broad ways to diversify your portfolio.

1. By asset class.

2. By geography.

Diversifying by asset class

Stocks have a higher expected return than bonds but are much more volatile. Bonds have historically been used as a hedge against the risk of a stock market crash.

During the financial crisis, the U.S. stock market fell by more than 40%. While during the same time period, bond prices increased.

Having a portion of your portfolio that increases in value during a market crash is one way to reduce your anxiety during times of uncertainty and avoid the "*sell-low, buy-high*" trap previously discussed.

For most investors, it makes sense to diversify your portfolio between stocks and bonds.

Choosing your asset allocation

One of the most critical decisions a DIY investor makes is how much of their portfolio to allocate toward risky assets like stocks and less volatile assets like bonds.

To determine how much of your portfolio should be in risky assets, like stocks, you need to consider two things:

1. Your ability to take on risk
2. Your willingness to take on risk

Your ability to take on risk is determined by how compromised your finances would be if the stock market suddenly crashed. Here are some checkpoints that would suggest you have the ability to take on a lot of risk when investing.

- You have 3–6 months in a cash emergency fund.
- You have strong job security.
- The money you are investing will not be needed for 10 or more years.
- You have little or no debt.

Your willingness to take on risk goes back to the issue of behavioral risk. Even if you are in a financial position to take on risk, you may not be psychologically prepared to watch your investments decline by 50% or more over a short period of time. If you have lived through a stock market crash in which you were invested at the time, think about how stressed you were during that period. That is your first data point to help determine your willingness to take on risk.

Vanguard has developed a free tool to help you answer that question[34]. This risk profile asks you a series of questions,

---

[34] *Vanguard - Investor Questionnaire - Terms and conditions of use.* (2021). Vanguard. https://retirementplans.vanguard.com/VGApp/pe/PubQuiz Activity?Step=start

and based on your results, it recommends an allocation to stocks and bonds that is appropriate for your risk tolerance.

Diversifying by geography

The second layer of portfolio diversification is to dedicate a portion of your portfolio in international investments.

If you invest all your money in a single country and that country's stock market suffers, you will have poor investment returns. If you have your money spread across multiple countries, even if one country is underperforming, that might be offset by another country outperforming.

A paper written by Vanguard in 2019 determined that investors who allocate roughly half of their portfolio to international stocks experience the least volatility compared to investors who only invest in stocks in their home county[35].

How much to allocate toward international and domestic?

The data and the theory demonstrate that it's probably a good idea for investors to have at least some exposure to international investments. The question is, how much?

One approach to decide how much your investments in stocks should be domestic vs. international is to base it off your home country's share of the global stock market.

---

[35] Vanguard Research. (2019, February). *Global equity investing: The benefits of diversification and sizing your allocation*. Vanguard.

For U.S. investors, that would mean investing roughly 55% of your investment in stocks in the U.S. and 45% internationally.

Beware of withholding taxes

An important consideration when investing in international index funds is withholding taxes. A withholding tax is the tax levied by a foreign government when an investor receives dividends from a company in that foreign country.

Withholding taxes vary by asset class and country. It is beyond the scope of this beginner's guide to dive too deeply into this complex subject.

Preferential tax treatments of investing domestically

While withholding taxes act as a disincentive to invest internationally, most governments provide tax incentives to invest in domestic stocks.

I am Canadian, so I will review the issue of tax incentives on domestic dividends from the perspective of a Canadian investor. Many other countries, including the U.S., provide a similar incentive to invest in domestic stocks.

When I invest in a Canadian stock index fund in a taxable account, the dividends paid to me are what are called "eligible dividends". These dividends receive a preferential tax treatment compared to dividends from an ETF that invests in international stocks.

I live in the province of Ontario in Canada, where the highest marginal tax rate is more than 53%. If I am in that 53% tax bracket, I would only pay a 39% tax on my "*eligible dividends*" I receive from publicly traded Canadian companies. Any dividends I receive from international companies would be taxed at 53%.

- If I received $10,000 in dividends from Canadian companies, I would have roughly $6,100 left after taxes.
- If I received $10,000 in dividends from foreign companies, I would have roughly $4,700 left after taxes.

This provides a powerful incentive for me to allocate more of my portfolio to domestic rather than international stocks.

How to think about international allocation

Investing internationally provides greater diversification to a portfolio, but it comes at the cost of withholding taxes and forgone tax incentives from investing in domestic stocks (when held in a taxable account.)

So, how much of your portfolio should be allocated to domestic and international stocks?

There is no one correct answer.

If dividends from domestic and international stocks were treated equally, the rational approach for the equity portion of your portfolio would be to invest in one index fund that tracks the global stock market and invests in each country based on that country's share of the global stock market.

- Think of this market-weighted approach as the starting point for your domestic vs. international allocation.

- Then consider the withholding taxes of investing internationally, which provides an incentive to invest more in domestic stocks.

- Then consider any tax incentives of investing domestically, which provides further incentive to invest in domestic stocks.

How much you invest domestically and internationally will depend on what country you live in and how you feel about the incentives I just described.

Robo-advisor or pure DIY?

No matter how much reading and research some people do, they simply don't feel comfortable managing their investments on their own. If that sounds like you, then perhaps you might consider using a robo-advisor to help you manage your investment portfolio.

A robo-advisor is an online platform to provide automated, algorithm-driven financial advice. The robo-advisor asks you questions about your goals, your risk tolerance, and other personal financial questions and constructs an investment portfolio for you based on the answers you provide.

Robo-advisors charge an annual fee, typically based on the amount of the assets it manages on your behalf. Whereas a "full-service" advisory firm might charge 1% or more per year, many robo-advisors charge as little as 0.25%.

Like with human advisors, it's important to do your homework and research different robo-advisors to find the one that fits your circumstances. Investopedia has put together a list of the most popular robo-advisors and listed the pros and cons of each[36].

Working with a robo-advisor can be an excellent choice for someone not comfortable building and managing an investment portfolio but does not want to work with a full-service financial advisor.

Important factors to consider when picking index ETFs

Once you know how much of your portfolio you need to allocate to domestic stocks, international stocks, domestic bonds, and international bonds, the next task for DIY investors is to choose ETFs that are the best fit for their portfolio.

---

[36] *Best Robo-Advisors.* (2021). Investopedia. https://www.investopedia.com/best-robo-advisors-4693125

If you are a U.S. investor and you need to buy a U.S. stock market index fund to satisfy the domestic stock allocation of your portfolio, how do you know which ETF to choose? There is an ever-increasing supply of ETFs that seemingly do the same thing, how can you possibly tell the difference?

Here are three things I look at when considering an ETF for my portfolio:

1. The Management Expense Ratio (MER).

2. Commissions.

3. Fund structure and withholding tax implications.

Let's briefly review each of these factors so you can understand their importance when selecting which ETFs to buy to construct your portfolio.

Management Expense Ratios

All index funds have one job: to replicate the returns of the index they are designed to track. There are many different S&P 500 index funds, and they all do the exact same thing: track the S&P 500 index.

Even though all index funds tracking a particular index have the same job, they have different fees. Index funds are a commodity product, and the worst decision you can make when selecting index ETFs is paying more fees than you need to.

An ETF Management Expense Ratio (MER) is a fee you pay to the fund which pays for all the costs of running the fund. MERs are a percentage of the money you have invested in the fund.

Whatever type of index fund I am considering, **the first thing I look for is the MER of the various funds that track that index.** If I am looking for an index fund that tracks the Canadian stock market, I pull up the various Canadian equity ETFs and start comparing the MER of each fund.

All else being equal, I go with the fund with the lowest MER.

Commissions

This issue has less to do with the ETF you choose and is more about which online broker you choose to buy your ETFs from.

Some online brokerages charge commission fees when you buy an ETF. These fees can be $5 or more per transaction. If you're starting out and only investing small amounts of money, these commissions can eat away at your portfolio.

It's important to find an online broker that charges low commissions for buying ETFs.

Fund structure & withholding taxes

We have already covered the fact that when you invest in stocks in foreign countries, you are likely going to pay withholding taxes on any dividends you receive.

It's important to consider how the ETF you are investing in is structured, as that could open you up to a second layer of withholding taxes, especially for investors outside of the U.S.

Broadly speaking, there are two ways ETFs that invest in international stocks can be structured:

1. The ETF holds the stocks directly.

2. The ETF invests in one or more other ETFs that hold international stocks.

As a Canadian, if I want to invest in international (outside of North America) stocks, I have very few choices of ETFs that are traded on the Canadian stock exchange that hold international stocks directly.

Most likely, I'll need to invest in an ETF listed on the Canadian stock exchange that owns ETFs listed on the U.S. stock exchange, which invests in international stocks.

In these cases, I am charged two levels of withholding taxes:

- The first layer of withholding taxes is applied by the foreign governments where the companies are located.

- The second layer of withholding taxes is applied by the U.S. government.

If possible, the goal when investing in international ETFs should be to avoid the second layer of withholding taxes.

What are the most popular index funds in DIY portfolios?

Let me be clear. I am not licensed to give recommendations on specific stocks or investment funds. That being said, I am happy to provide you with a list of some of the most popular index funds that DIY investors use to build their portfolio.

Any fund included on the list does not imply an endorsement of the fund, and I have no affiliation with any of these fund companies. This is simply a resource to get you started.

The ticker name for each fund will appear in brackets.

U.S. stock market index funds

- Vanguard S&P 500 index fund (VOO).

- Vanguard Total stock market index fund (VTI).

- iShares S&P 500 index fund (IVV).

- iShares total stock market index fund (ITOT).

International stock market index funds

- Vanguard total international stock fund (VXUS).

- Vanguard FTSE Developed Markets fund (VEA).

- Vanguard emerging markets fund (VWO).

- iShares core MSCI total international stock fund (IXUS).

- iShares core MSCI developed markets international stock fund (IXUS).

- iShares core MSCI emerging markets stock fund (IDEV).

U.S. bond market index funds

- Vanguard total bond market fund (BND).

- iShares total U.S bond market fund (IUSB).

International bond market index funds

- Vanguard total international bond fund (BNDX)

- iShares core international aggregate bond fund (IAGG).

Building your ETF portfolio

To build your portfolio of ETFs requires you to select the right ETFs to achieve your desired allocation to stocks and bonds as well as your allocation between domestic and international investments.

For example, let's say a U.S. DIY investor wants to build a portfolio that is 50% bonds and 50% stocks. For simple math, let's also assume they want a 50–50 split between domestic and international stocks and bonds. The investor would need to select ETFs that satisfy the following requirements:

- 25% of the total portfolio in U.S. stock index funds.

- 25% of the total portfolio in international stock index funds.

- 25% of the total portfolio in U.S. bond index funds.

- 25% of the total portfolio in international bond index funds.

The more complex the portfolio, the more work is involved in building and maintaining the portfolio. Don't forget, you'll also need to rebalance your portfolio on occasion if you want to maintain your desired allocations.

It's worth repeating that if this sounds too intimidating, you can always choose a robo-advisor, which can help you with the construction and rebalancing of a portfolio of index ETFs.

Is it possible to properly diversify by investing in only one or two ETFs?

Yes, it is absolutely possible to build a diversified portfolio using two or even one ETF.

To build a diversified portfolio using two ETFs, you could simply invest in an ETF that tracks the global stock market and an ETF that tracks the global bond market.

- An example of a globally diversified stock ETF would be Vanguard's total world stock ETF (VT).

- An example of a globally diversified bond ETF would be Vanguard's total world bond ETF (BNDW)

It's also possible to invest in a single ETF that provides you a ready-made diversified portfolio.

For example, Vanguard's balanced index fund (VBINX) provides you with a one ETF portfolio that invests in 60% stocks and 40% bonds. There are different "one fund solutions" for more or less aggressive asset allocations.

When you're just getting started with investing, it's important to embrace simplicity. That is why I like the idea of one or two ETF portfolios. The fewer decisions you have to make, the more successful you are likely to be as an investor.

Chapter Recap

- Index funds are investment funds that replicate an index of assets like stocks or bonds.

- ETFs are investment funds that can be bought on a stock exchange like a stock.

- Not all index funds are ETFs, and not all ETFs are index funds.

- There are generally two types of index funds; broad-based index funds and niche index funds.

- Broad-based index funds are a rational way to invest because they are simple, have low investment fees, and are extremely diversified.

- To diversify your portfolio, think about diversifying both by asset class and geography.

- You can use risk assessment tools to gain a sense of the right allocation to stocks and bonds.

- Make sure to take foreign withholding taxes and preferential tax treatment for domestic dividends when considering your allocation between domestic and international ETFs.

- Once you have an idea of your allocations, you'll need to select the ETFs that match your desired allocations to stocks and bonds and domestic and international investments.

- Remember, index funds that track a particular index all have the same job, so all else being equal, selecting the ETF with the lowest annual fees will save you money.

- Buying ETFs on your own can feel intimidating, but all you need is to know some basic terminology and get some experience.

- If building and maintaining an index ETF portfolio is intimidating, you can always choose to work with a robo-advisor that takes care of building and rebalancing your portfolio for you.

Chapter 16:

What About Real Estate?

You may have noticed that in our discussion about passive investing, the issue of real estate is conspicuously absent.

You might think this an odd choice because real estate investing has become synonymous with passive income. The odds are that before you found this book, you scrolled past a number of different books equating real estate with financial freedom and passive income.

In this chapter I want to make three things abundantly clear about real estate"

1. It can help you achieve financial freedom.

2. Investing in real estate is not passive.

3. Owning rental properties is not for everyone.

Allow me to make the case as to why real estate is one of the most overrated investment ideas.

Real estate has become a cultural obsession

In 2018, there were more than 13 billion Google search queries for real estate.

If you're an American between the age of 50–64, there is a 31% chance you have watched at least one Home & Garden Television (HGTV) show in the past month.

55% of Millennials surveyed said they wanted to invest in real estate.

Nearly everyone I know seems to love the idea of investing in real estate. I include myself in that statement. I am the son of two real estate agents and have long been obsessed with the idea of owning real estate.

I'll say at the top that I have invested in real estate, and I have made money doing so. I currently own more than $1.1 million in real estate assets. Real estate has been good to me, but it's far from perfect.

I am not making the case that real estate investing is bad. Real estate is a very solid asset class that has a place in many investment portfolios.

However, real estate is the most overrated asset in history. Our cultural obsession with real estate has put the asset class on a pedestal it could never live up to.

The media has glorified real estate investing

On HGTV alone, there are well over 100 TV shows centred around real estate. These shows cover every possible real estate niche.

- Buying homes
- Selling homes

- Renovating homes
- Flipping houses
- Building custom decks
- Buying real estate in foreign countries
- Summer homes and cottages
- Buying income properties
- "Tiny" homes
- "Dream" homes
- Real estate agent shows

Within each of these niches, there are multiple shows centred in different real estate markets.

If you want a show about flipping houses in Las Vegas, it's there.

If you want a show about DIY home repairs in Chicago, it's there too.

Do you know why a single network has over 100 real estate-related TV shows? Because people love these shows. Whether you live in a big city or rural community, liberal or conservative, young or old, we are all united by our obsession with real estate.

I'll say it again; this applies to me too. I have probably watched at least a dozen real estate-related shows with my wife over the past few years. Whenever I watch one of these shows, I can't help but have the same thought that everyone else has; "I should be doing this."

How the stock market is portrayed in the media

There are entire networks that cover what happens in the stock market. Networks like Bloomberg and CNBC provide live news coverage and commentary on what is happening in the stock market.

Unlike HGTV, there is nothing "fun" about stock market coverage.

Few people have ever binge-watched three hours of stock market coverage and thought to themselves, "I should be doing this."

There are several popular movies centred around the stock market. Three movies, in particular, come to mind.

- 1987's "Wall Street" in which the most memorable moment of the movie is when the movie's villain, Gordon Gekko, declares that "greed is good."

- 2013's "The Wolf of Wall Street" highlights how depraved and sleazy some Wall Street traders can be.

- 2015's "The Big Short" recounts how fraudulent practices within the mortgage securities industry nearly brought the world into another great depression.

If you watch stock market coverage on TV, you will be bored out of your mind.

If you watch movies centred around Wall Street and the stock market, you are likely to come away with the feeling that investing in the stock market is dirty and perhaps even immoral.

Contrast that with the feeling you get when you watch real estate shows on HGTV, and you can understand why everyone is obsessed with real estate and why so few people are invested in the stock market.

But here's the truth.

For most people, stocks are a better investment than real estate

When you adjust for risk, effort, and time, investing in the stock market is hands down a better option for most people than investing in physical real estate.

To illustrate why stocks can be a better option, I will compare investing in physical real estate to investing in Vanguards Total World Stock Market Index Fund. This fund tracks the global stock market. This is not an endorsement to invest in this particular fund, but I'll use it to illustrate the simplicity of investing in stocks compared to real estate.

It's impossible to properly diversify with real estate

In each of the markets I own property in, it would cost you upwards of $500,000 to acquire a single property.

Spending hundreds of thousands of dollars on a single property, in a single neighborhood, in a single city, in a single state or province, in a single country makes it virtually impossible for regular people to diversify their real estate portfolio.

By contrast, with a total world stock market index fund, I can invest in more than 8,400 companies across the planet. The cost per unit? $64.

Investing in real estate is the definition of putting all your eggs in one basket.

If you own a single property and something happens to that property or your tenants are not able to pay the rent, the income will stop coming in, but the mortgage still needs to get paid.

Real estate has a lot of operational costs

Unlike investing in stocks, real estate is an investment that you have to continue throwing time and money at.

- When you buy a property, be prepared to pay between 2%-5% of the purchase price of the property in closing costs.

- Every year you will need to pay property taxes which, as a rule of thumb, are about 1% of the value of the property.

- You also need to budget for constant maintenance costs. Another rule of thumb is to budget for at least 1% of the value of the property in annual maintenance costs.

- If you own a property, you also need to pay for insurance, which can run about $1,500 per year.

- Vacancy costs. Your rental property is not going to be occupied with a tenant every single month you own it. There will be months where you have no tenant paying you rent, but you still need to pay the bills associated with the property.

- If you choose to have a property manager, be prepared to fork over between 8%-12% of the monthly rent.

- Don't forget the mortgage. If you buy the property using debt, you'll need to pay the principal and interest each month.

Ideally, the tenant would cover all these costs through the monthly rent. However, all of these costs eat into the income generated from the property.

By contrast, investing $100,000 in the global index fund would cost about $80 per year in investment management costs.

Residential real estate is a highly regulated industry

Regulatory risk is one of the greatest risks facing a landlord. To you, real estate is an investment. To your tenant, it is their home.

That comes with a lot of responsibility; if you are a bad landlord, it makes life hard for your tenants.

Since this is such an important responsibility, the government often steps in with laws and regulations surrounding the landlord-tenant relationship.

If you currently live in a city where the laws and regulations favor the tenant, the greater the risk to you as a landlord. You could find yourself in a situation where your tenant is not paying rent, and you cannot get a new tenant for months.

Even if you live in a city where laws and regulations favor the landlord, that is something that could change at any time.

These types of regulatory risks are not something that you need to worry about investing in the stock market.

Real estate investing is not passive

Unless you are using a property manager, investing in real estate requires a lot of work.

- Finding a property to invest in.
- Finding an agent and mortgage broker you can trust.
- Negotiating an offer to purchase the property.
- Obtaining financing at a rate that will allow you to produce positive cash flow.

- Inspecting the property before closing.

- Dealing with lawyers before closing.

- Finding a contractor that you can trust to take care of any rehabs and repairs required.

- Advertising that the property is available for rent.

- Screening tenants and running credit checks.

- Collecting rent every month.

- Evicting tenants if need be (something nobody wants to do).

- Calling plumbers and contractors when maintenance is required.

- Paying the property tax bills.

The list goes on and on, but I think you get the point.

If you are self-managing your real estate portfolio, you don't have a passive investment; you have a business. Your return on investment with real estate is directly linked to your skill at finding deals, finding tenants, and managing the property. This is the most important thing you need to know about real estate. It can lead to financial freedom, but only if you are a skilled real estate investor. If you make terrible decisions, you could lose your shirt in real estate.

Compare that to investing in a globally diversified index fund; you invest, and then you do nothing.

In fact, you don't even need to check your investment account or follow the day-to-day movements in the stock market. When you invest for the long-term using index funds, the less involved you are, the better your returns are likely to be.

Index funds are a passive investment; real estate is not.

Even if you understand and agree with everything I just said, the odds are that you still have the "real estate bug." I am as guilty as anyone for having a bias towards real estate. If you decide that you simply must own real estate, let's review a more rational way to invest

Real Estate Investment Trusts (REITs): The passive way to invest in real estate

REITs are companies that invest in commercial real estate. REITs invest in a variety of Real Estate projects that most regular people would not have the capital to invest in, such as:

- Large apartment complexes
- Office buildings
- Healthcare facilities
- Retirement facilities
- Shopping malls
- Retail plazas
- Industrial buildings
- Factories, warehouses, and other industrial buildings

For every type of property you can think of; there is likely a REIT that invests in it.

How to buy REITs

There are two types of REITs

1. Private REITs

2. Public REITs

I have never invested in private REITs, so for the remainder of this discussion, I am referring to public REITs when I talk about REITs.

They are called public REITs because they are publicly traded on the stock exchange, where investors can purchase shares of REITs in the same way you would buy shares of Apple, Amazon, or any other publicly traded company.

Why I prefer REITs to physical real estate

While I do own physical real estate, moving forward, all my investments in real estate will be through REITs. I am choosing to do this because REITs solve the three most significant investing problems in physical real estate.

#1 Diversification. Rather than investing in one property in one city with physical real estate, REITs allow me to invest in thousands of different properties in different geographical locations.

#2 Liquidity. Selling a physical property takes a long time (often months) and a lot of money through paying a real estate agent, lawyers, and other fees. In addition to that, selling physical real estate is an all-or-nothing proposition. I can't sell half of a property. All of those issues go away with REITs, where I can instantly sell anywhere between 0%-100% of my investment in REITs for only a few dollars in fees.

#3 The time required to manage properties. If you own and operate your rental properties, that involves a lot of work to manage them. You can pay a property manager to help with those duties, but there is no escaping the fact that owning physical real estate requires a time commitment. REITs, on the other hand, are a truly passive investment.

REITs are risky

One of the most common misconceptions about REITs is that they are somehow less risky than traditional stocks. While the volatility of REITs has been slightly lower than stocks, make no mistake investing in REITs involves a high degree of risk.

Since investing in REITs is an investment in one sector of the economy (real estate), it exposes them to idiosyncratic risk. Meaning REITs are exposed to the specific risks facing the real estate sector of the economy.

If you think about the last two recessions, they hit different aspects of the real estate sector very hard.

- In 2020, as people began sheltering in place at home, many parts of the real estate sector were hit hard. In particular, retail, shopping malls, and office buildings.

- The financial crisis of 2008/2009 was triggered in the residential real estate mortgage market.

In both cases, real estate and REITs were hit hard. REITs are risky assets and can be just as volatile as stocks, with the additional caveat that they expose investors to the idiosyncratic risk of the real estate sector.

How I invest in REITs

Another misconception about REITs is that many compare investing in an individual REIT as being the same thing as investing in a "mutual fund for real estate." Someone making this argument would point out the similarities between individual REITs and mutual funds.

- Both employ a manager to choose the assets to invest in.
- Both provide greater diversification by investing in a large pool of assets.

To be clear, investing in individual REITs is not the same as investing in a mutual fund or index fund. Investing in individual REITs is no different than investing in individual stocks.

225 REITs trade publicly in the U.S alone. Many of these REITs specialize in investing in a specific type of property, for example, apartment buildings or office buildings.

Investing in an individual REITs opens you up to further idiosyncratic risk. If you invest in a REIT that specializes in buying office buildings in three different cities, you are exposed not only to the risk in the entire real estate market but also the risk of the specific office building sector and the specific economic conditions in the three cities that REIT invests in.

In the same way, I buy index funds when I invest in stocks and bonds; I buy index funds to invest in REITs. Investing in a REIT index fund removes the city and industry-specific risks of individual REITs. Why buy one or two specialized REITs when I can own them all?

Where I invest in REITs

An important consideration is where to hold investments in REITs.

Another crucial difference between REITs and traditional stocks is how the dividends from each investment are taxed.

In Canada and the U.S, dividends from publicly traded domestic companies are given preferential tax treatment.

The distribution from REITs, on the other hand, has a more complex tax treatment. Often times are often taxed as regular income but can also be taxed as qualified dividends in the U.S, in which case they would be taxed as capital gains. Do your research on tax implications before investing in REITs.

For that reason, I invest in REITs in my retirement and other tax-sheltered accounts. Investing in REITs in a taxable investment account would be inefficient as I would be paying significantly more in taxes on my investment returns.

Chapter recap

- Most people invest in what they feel comfortable with.

- Due to our cultural obsession with real estate, many more people feel comfortable investing in real estate than they do investing in the stock market.

- The ironic truth is that investing in real estate requires taking on more risk by taking out a mortgage and going into debt to invest in a property.

- Real estate investing also requires a lot more effort and has a lot more ongoing expenses compared to investing in a low-cost index fund.

- REITs solve the diversification, cost and management issues facing physical real estate.

- REITs are companies that invest in commercial real estate and return the profits to shareholders.

- REITs can be further diversified by buying an ETF that tracks the entire market for REITs.

Chapter 17:

If You Want Financial Freedom, You Must Fight Lifestyle Inflation

Your boss calls you into his office and tells you that you have been promoted. You'll be getting an impressive title, a corner office, and of course, a big fat pay raise. Upon hearing this news, you go back to your desk and start making plans to buy that sports car you have always dreamed of owning but couldn't afford until now.

That is lifestyle inflation.

Put in the simplest possible terms, lifestyle inflation refers to the phenomenon of your cost of living increasing alongside your income. As more money goes in, more money goes out.

It seems harmless, and after all, why shouldn't you enjoy some of the finer things in life when you get a raise? It's very easy to tell ourselves that we have worked hard and deserve to own fancier, more expensive stuff.

The truth is that lifestyle inflation is one of the great destroyers of wealth and is what will prevent many people from achieving financial freedom.

To understand why, refer back to the financial freedom equation:

Financial Freedom= (Income from work you love + Passive income) > Your living expenses

If your living expenses keep increasing, financial freedom gets further away.

The psychological trap of lifestyle inflation

If you want to avoid falling into the trap of lifestyle inflation, it's useful to examine its root cause. There are endless excuses (and I have heard a lot of them) that people would use to justify their overspending. **It all boils down to the simple need to project a certain level of social status.**

When you look at the big-ticket items that people overspend on, you will notice that they are all *visible* expenses.

- Big houses
- Luxury cars
- Lavish vacations (with lots of pictures for the Gram)
- Designer clothes
- Jewellery and watches

All these expenses scream to the world, "*look at me, I made it!*"

The original term for this need to spend to impress was called *"keeping up with the Joneses"*. If your neighbors, let's call them "*the Joneses*", bought a brand-new BMW, you might start looking at your 5-year-old Toyota in the driveway and begin to feel a bit insecure. Maybe that causes you to go out and buy a new car that is just as nice or even better than your neighbor's BMW.

The sad reality is that we all have a natural tendency to compare ourselves to other people. A paper written by Ada Ferrer-i-Carbonellin published in the Journal of Public Economics[37] found that people's happiness and sense of self-worth are equally impacted by two factors.

1. How much money they make.

2. How much money the people around them make.

People who know that they make more money than their friends and neighbors are the most likely to feel successful with money. This is referred to as "*social comparison*", which is the root cause of lifestyle inflation.

Social media spreads lifestyle inflation like wildfire

If you didn't know that your friends and family had more money than you do, the odds are you would feel better about your financial situation and would not feel the pressure to give in to lifestyle inflation.

[37] Ferrer-i-Carbonell, A. (2005). Income and well-being: an empirical analysis of the comparison income effect. *Journal of Public Economics*, *89*(5–6), 997–1019. https://doi.org/10.1016/j.jpubeco.2004.06.003

The solution should seem obvious; focus on your finances and don't worry about what everyone else is doing. Unfortunately, in the era of social media, that is close to impossible.

Most people use social media to paint themselves in the best possible light. If you were to scroll through most of your friend's Instagram feeds, you would find pictures of them on epic vacations, eating at the best restaurants, and dressed to the nines.

What you would not see is pictures of them eating in front of the TV with a mustard stain on their shirts. Even if the mustard stain is more representative of their day-to-day life.

People also use social media to make themselves look more financially successful than they really are. No one wants to broadcast that they have three maxed-out credit cards and are living paycheck to paycheck. Instead, they post pictures that give the impression that they are wealthy and successful. A report called "The Secret Financial Life of Americans[38]" found that 28% of Millennials admitted that they intentionally try to make themselves look wealthier than they really are through social media.

This is where social media amplifies social comparison and pushes people toward lifestyle inflation. When you

---

[38] Scarfo, G., & Zeidler, B. (2018, January). *THE SECRET FINANCIAL LIVES OF AMERICANS*. Non Fiction.

see pictures of people you know who appear to be so much more successful than you, you are more likely to feel worse about your financial situation.

If you see a picture of your buddy Bryan on a beach in some exotic destination, you are more likely to feel the pressure to book your own trip, even if you can't afford it. Then it's your turn to post some "epic" picture that will cause your friends to feel like they are missing out or failing somehow.

Social media makes us all feel miserable and pushes us to spend money we don't have on things we don't need.

How to end the destructive cycle of lifestyle inflation

Lifestyle inflation is a psychological problem and requires a psychological solution. This is not something you can fix with a spreadsheet.

The lure of lifestyle inflation is always present, you simply need to fight against its pull. That's why you need a strong, confident mindset to win the daily battle with lifestyle inflation.

The first step to building a strong money mindset is to have a "*why*"—a motivation that is more powerful than the temptation to give in to lifestyle inflation. There is a reason we covered this topic in the first chapter of this book. If you find the right "why", you will be able to resist the pull of lifestyle inflation.

What to do when you get a pay raise

Here's a simple trick you can use to ensure you never fall victim to lifestyle inflation.

The next time you get a pay raise, work out how much more money you will clear on every paycheck, and set up an automatic savings plan for that money. For example, if you got a pay raise that would increase your take-home pay by $100 every two weeks, you would call your bank and set up an automatic transfer into a savings account every two weeks.

When I say savings, this could be for many things:

- Saving for an emergency fund.
- Retirement savings.
- Investing.
- Paying off debt.
- Saving for your child's education.

The most important thing is that you automate the process. It takes the decision out of your hand and guarantees that you don't fall victim to lifestyle inflation.

Remember, a high income does not make someone wealthy, and a low income does not make someone poor. It is about what you save, not what you make. That is why it is crucial to keep lifestyle inflation in check.

Chapter recap

- Spending more money as our income increases can seem harmless at first, but it slowly weakens your financial security over time. Once your paycheck stops coming in, you will feel the devastating consequences of lifestyle inflation.

- If you want to avoid lifestyle inflation, you must have a "*why*" that is more powerful than the pull of lifestyle inflation.

- If you simply automate your raises into a savings account every payday, you will be able to spare yourself from falling back into lifestyle inflation.

Chapter 18:

The 10% Rule: How to Reach Financial Freedom in Less Than 10 Years

It's time to tie everything together and provide a clear road map for achieving financial freedom, which as a reminder, I define as:

Spending your days doing work that you love without worrying about how you will pay the bills.

The best part of this definition of financial freedom is that it does not require you to amass a massive amount of wealth. It simply requires you to find a way to pay for all your living expenses, plus a little extra for retirement savings, by doing work that you truly love.

By that definition, an artist making $38,000 per year could have more financial freedom than an investment banker making $380,000 per year.

In this chapter, I review how anyone can achieve financial freedom in less than 10 years using what I call "the 10% rule". I'll also review some tips on how you can speed up your timeline to financial freedom, even if you are starting from scratch.

The 10% Rule

The most important factor that will determine how long it takes to achieve financial freedom is **the amount of money you can make doing work you love relative to your living expenses**.

If you have a 9–5 job that you don't love, the only path to financial freedom is finding work that you love and are truly passionate about.

That does NOT mean you should go out and quit your job. The income from your job can provide financial security for you and your family, and that is not something you should take for granted.

Instead of quitting your job, why not pick up a side-hustle? We have already discussed the importance of having multiple income streams. I want to emphasize how important it is that you choose a side hustle doing work that you love.

Which brings me to the 10% rule:

If every year you can replace an additional 10% of your current income doing work you love, you can achieve financial freedom in no more than 10 years.

How to figure out exactly when you'll be financially free following the 10% rule.

The easiest way to understand how the 10% rule works is with an example.

Let's assume the following:

- You have a corporate job that pays you $70,000 per year.

- After taxes and deductions, your annual take-home pay is $48,000.

- Your annual expenses are equal to 90% of your take-home pay or $43,200.

- Each year, your take-home pay and your expenses rise by 2%.

- Maybe you love cooking. Being in the kitchen and preparing fantastic dishes for you and others to enjoy is one of your favorite things to do. So, you pick up a side hustle writing and making videos about cooking recipes.

- Your goal in the first year of launching your cooking side hustle is to replace 10% of your take-home pay or $4,800.

- In your second year, your goal is to replace 20% of your take-home pay (which has increased by 2%) for a total of $9,792 with your side hustle.

- Each year you scale the income of your side hustle to replace an additional 10% of the take-home pay your day job provides you.

- After year nine, the income you receive from your side hustle and your annual expenses are equal at $50,616.

This is summarized in the following table:

Year	Annual Take home pay	Annual Expenses	Income from a side hustle you love	Percentage of income from day job
1	$ 48,000	$ 43,200	$ 4,800	10%
2	$ 48,960	$ 44,064	$ 9,792	20%
3	$ 49,939	$ 44,945	$ 14,982	30%
4	$ 50,938	$ 45,844	$ 20,375	40%
5	$ 51,957	$ 46,761	$ 25,978	50%
6	$ 52,996	$ 47,696	$ 31,798	60%
7	$ 54,056	$ 48,650	$ 37,839	70%
8	$ 55,137	$ 49,623	$ 44,110	80%
9	$ 56,240	$ 50,616	$ 50,616	90%
10	$ 57,364	$ 51,628	$ 57,364	100%

When you can cover all your living expenses doing work you love, you have achieved financial freedom.

To be clear, to make sure you are comparing apples to apples, the income you earn from your side hustle should be calculated net of taxes because it is replacing your net income from your day job.

Living frugally will dramatically reduce your timeline to financial freedom

If nine years sounds like a really long time, then I have good news; *you don't have to wait nine years.*

Remember, the point of financial freedom is when you can cover all your living expenses with income from doing work you love (plus passive investment income). You do not need to replace all the income from your day job or even 90% of it.

In the example above, where it took nine years to achieve financial freedom, we assumed that, in year one, your living expenses were 90% of your take-home pay.

The lower your living expenses are as a percentage of your take-home pay, the less of your current income you'll need to replace from your side hustle.

- If your living expenses are 80% of your take-home pay, you can achieve financial freedom in 8 years.

- If your living expenses are 70% of your take-home pay, you can achieve financial freedom in 7 years.

Assuming you can replace an additional 10% of your take-home pay every year through your side hustle, the lower your living expenses are, the faster you will achieve financial freedom.

This is summarized in the following chart:

EXPENSES AS A % OF TAKE-HOME PAY	YEARS UNTIL FINANCIAL FREEDOM
100%	10
90%	9
80%	8
70%	7
60%	6
50%	5
40%	4
30%	3
20%	2
0%	1

The faster you can scale your income, the faster you'll achieve financial freedom

The 10% rule assumes that you are replacing an additional 10% of the income from your day job with your side hustle or passion project each year. I picked 10% for two reasons:

1. It sets realistic expectations (it can take a long time to make real money pursuing your passions).

2. 10% is a round number, and people like round numbers.

My point is that there is nothing magical about 10%. If you can replace more than 10% of the income you make from your day job each year, you will achieve financial freedom much faster.

The only magic number is the difference between your annual expenses and net income generated from doing work you love. Once that number is $0, you have achieved financial freedom.

What counts as "living expenses"?

I keep using the term *living expenses,* but what exactly do I mean by that?

This is simple: we will consider living expenses to include literally any transaction where money leaves your pocket or your bank account.

-   That means all your traditional living expenses like housing, food, transportation, entertainment, travel, etc.

- Seasonal spending on things like birthdays and holidays.

- It also includes any short-term savings, for example, money put into an emergency fund, house repair fund, or a travel fund.

- Finally, it will include a basic amount for how much you need to save and invest for long-term retirement planning.

Yes, you need to include an allotment for retirement savings. If you're doing work you love, you might think, "*I never need to retire*". But here's the thing, it may not be up to you.

By the time you reach traditional retirement age, your health or the state of the economy may not allow you to continue working. Therefore, you need to be able to save a basic amount for retirement from your side hustle before you can be considered financially free. So, once you can cover all your living expenses and savings requirements from income generated doing something you love, you are financially free.

Financial freedom is not a lifetime guarantee

Since Financial Freedom is dependent on the income you can generate from doing something you love, it is a fluid situation. Achieving financial freedom does not guarantee you a lifetime of freedom.

If you can no longer generate enough income to cover your expenses from doing work you love, you could lose your financial freedom.

This could be a temporary situation if you have a few bad earning months, or it could be a permanent situation in which case you would need to pick up either part-time or full-time work at a 9-to-5 that you may not "love" but need to keep paying the bills.

That is why many people would not choose to actually "claim" their financial freedom as soon as their side-hustle income surpasses their living expenses.

I would count myself among that group of people. My side-hustle generates enough income to cover most of my living expenses, but I am very happy to continue working a great 9-to-5 that I like to help me accumulate more assets and give myself a bigger cushion.

Right now, I take every penny I earn from my side-hustle and invest it. As my portfolio builds, it begins to produce its own income, which could help supplement my side-hustle income in lean months if I ever choose to grab financial freedom and make my side-hustle my main hustle.

It's not going to be easy, and there is no guarantee of success, but you need to know that it is absolutely possible for you to achieve financial freedom one day. Start with the first step of replacing 10% of your income from doing work that you love and build on that success.

Chapter 19:

Should you claim Financial Freedom As Soon As You Can?

Let's end our journey where we began with the financial freedom equation.

Financial freedom= (Investment income + income from work you love) > Your living expenses

In this book, you've been given the road map to achieving that definition of financial freedom, from basic money management to passive investing to leveraging your skills and passions into a side hustle that generates positive cash flow.

We have one more topic left to tackle.

Should you claim financial freedom and quit your 9-5 job as soon as you satisfy the financial freedom equation? Should you call it quits as soon as your side hustle and investment income is enough to cover your living expenses?

It depends.

Let's review some of the questions you should ask yourself before pulling the trigger on financial freedom and quitting your day job.

You've become financially bulletproof. Do you want to give that up right away?

Once you have two income streams that could each pay for your desired lifestyle, you have a financial superpower.

It becomes nearly impossible to ever go broke for as long as you hold onto each of these income streams. If you lose your job or your side hustle went into the tank, you would be fine. That's because you have another source of income that picks up the slack without missing a beat (or a bill payment.)

This is diversification in action. Not diversification of an investment portfolio but diversification of your human capital.

A 9–5 job is the bond component of human capital. You receive the same payment at the same frequency (adjusted for inflation) without fail. Boring, reliable income with limited growth potential. A perfect definition of what a bond is.

The income you earn from a side hustle or side business has huge growth potential over time, but it's extremely volatile.

You might not have any problem with that type of volatility your side hustle right now because you have a steady, boring, bond-like income from your 9–5 to smooth out the down months.

So, before you ditch your 9-5, ask yourself two questions:

1. How volatile is the income from the work you love?

2. How stressed would you be if this was your only income source?

How much passive investment income do you have?

Remember, the only source of "passive income" is income generated from passively managed investments. Think dividends from stocks or interest from bonds.

The hard truth about passive investment income is that it takes most people a lifetime to build up enough of it to cover their living expenses.

Let's say your desired lifestyle costs you $40,00 per year. Let's also assume your investments yielded 3.5% per year. That means you would need $1,143,000 invested to cover your desired lifestyle with passive income. If you were saving $10,000 per year, it would take 38 years to achieve that goal.

If you can fund your lifestyle with your 9–5, that allows you to invest 100% of your side hustle income. That, in turn, helps you build a larger investment portfolio relative to your cost of living in a fraction of the time.

Let's assume the following.

- After tax income from 9–5 = $50,000
- After tax income from side-hustle=$40,000
- Desired lifestyle =$40,000.

Working just the 9–5 job would allow you to build enough passive income to cover your living expenses in 38 years.

Working just the side hustle wouldn't leave you any room to invest, so you are essentially stuck in a situation where you need to work forever if you can't scale your side hustle income.

But, working both the 9–5 and the side hustle allows you to invest $50,000 per year ($10,000 from the 9–5 and $40,000 from the side hustle.) This would cut down the time it would take to generate $40,000 in investment income from 38 years to 15 years.

I'm not saying you need enough passive income to cover all of your living expenses before you start doing work you love full-time. But, the more investment income you have, the more likely it is that you'll be able to withstand a few bad months of earning.

Another crucial lesson for anyone who wants to pursue their passion full-time is that your "cost of living" needs to include some amount of retirement savings. Because no matter how much you love the work you do, you need to provide yourself at least the option to stop working in your golden years.

Do you like your job?

This might be the most important factor to consider. Do you like your job, tolerate your job or hate your job?

If you like your 9-5 job, and your employer provides you flexibility like working from home, you may not be in a hurry to give up that job the second it becomes an option. Maybe it makes sense to continue working the side-hustle and 9-5 job as long as you can make it work so that you build up a larger base of financial capital.

Don't underestimate how comforting it is to choose to continue working a job when you have the option of quitting whenever you like. You've just taken real control over your life; you might want to spend some time wielding that power.

If you hate your job or find that it's having negative impacts on your 9-5, then it might make sense to quit as soon as you satisfy the variables of the financial freedom equation. There is no point in building F-U money if you're not prepared to say "F-U" to a situation that makes you miserable.

What would happen if your side hustle fell apart completely?

A side hustle or a side business can be more than volatile; sometimes, businesses fail completely and never recover.

If your business failed and you lost your income, you might need to (at least temporarily) find another job to cover your expenses again. Remember, financial freedom is not a lifelong guarantee. Before you quit your 9–5, you need enough money in cash to pay for your lifestyle until you find a new job. This takes a lot of the financially devastating consequences of your side-hustle falling off the table.

We covered this topic at great length in the chapter on emergency funds, so go back and read that chapter for a refresher on building your emergency fund. But here's a 3-step approach to determine the **minimum** amount of cash you need before dropping your 9–5.

1. Track your average monthly living expenses.

2. Research your industry and come up with a conservative estimate of how many months it would take to land a good job in your field.

3. Multiply your average monthly expenses by the number of months to find a new job.

If you spend $5,000 per month and a conservative estimate for how long it would take to find a new job is six months, then you need at least $30,000 in cash before quitting your job to pursue your side hustle full-time.

Chapter Recap

- Financial freedom is achieved when your income from work you love + investments are greater than your desired living expenses.

- The more passive investment income you have, the more margin of error you build into your post-financial-freedom life.

- Having multiple, uncorrelated streams of income makes you financially bulletproof.

- How much you enjoy—or hate—your job will be a critical variable when deciding when you should take your side hustle full time.

- Before quitting your 9-5 job, ensure you have enough cash in an emergency fund to cover your living expenses long enough for you to land a new job in the event that your side hustle goes to $0.

About The Author

Ben Le Fort is a personal finance writer and creator of the online publication "Making of a Millionaire." He has been passionate about personal finance ever since graduating University with $50,000+ in debt. In the eight years following graduation, he paid off all of the debt and built a seven-figure net worth. Ben holds a Bachelor's degree in economics from Acadia University and a Master's degree in Economics & Finance from The University of Guelph.

He lives in Waterloo, Ontario with his wife, son and cat named Trixie.

ONE LAST THING...

Thank you so much for reading this book. I poured a lot of sweat and tears into it.

Could you do me a favor? Please review this book on Amazon. Whether you thought it was great, terrible, or anywhere in between, I'd love to have your feedback.

Reviews are the best way for an author like me to get discovered. Readers like you can help make it happen.

Thanks in advance,

Ben